TRADITIONAL ENGLISH PRESERVES

by
Peggy Hutchinson

foulsham
London · New York · Toronto · Sydney

foulsham

The Publishing House, Bennetts Close,
Cippenham, Slough, Berkshire, SL1 5AP

ISBN 0-572-02136-4

Printed in Great Britain by
Cox & Wayman Ltd; Reading

CONTENTS

INTRODUCTION

A well-stocked store cupboard is the aim of every housewife, and it can be fun and rewarding to supplement your bought groceries with jars of jam, marmalade and jelly, bottles of fruit, pickles, chutneys and sauces which you have produced yourself. There can be sauces for special occasions, fruit mincemeat for Christmas, and even home-made beauty treatments. Today's housewife can also use a freezer to take care of raw materials from the garden and market, with the result that far less time need be spent in shopping and far more can be spent in more pleasurable gardening or cooking.

Even a small garden can hold enough fruit and vegetables for eating fresh and for preserving, while there are many fruits to be picked from the hedgerows during family expeditions. Many farms now offer a 'pick your own' service so that everyone can enjoy gathering food which will provide a full store-cupboard for the winter.

JAMS AND CURDS

Jams and curds can be easily made from fruit and sugar with very simple equipment. A large pan is necessary so that the jam can be boiled rapidly without boiling over, if you are fortunate enough to own one, a preserving pan is obviously ideal, but any large steel, aluminium or non-stick pan is fine. Chipped enamel should never be used and copper can spoil the colour of red fruit. Use a long-handled wooden spoon for stirring so that hot jam does not splash on to the hands.

It is a good idea to collect jam jars throughout the year. Honey jars, coffee jars and preserving jars are also suitable for potting jam, and they should be completely clean before use. Sterilise them by leaving the clean jars in the oven on its lowest setting for 30 minutes. When the jam has been put into each jar, cover it with a waxed disc as this will help to keep the jam well and give it a neat appearance. A transparent cover and a label with the type and date will complete each jar.

Ingredients

Fruit for jam-making should be fresh, sound and not mushy, and it is best slightly under-ripe as very ripe fruit has a reduced sugar content which will affect the setting and keeping quality of the jam. Some fruits need the addition of acid such as lemon juice or redcurrant juice to extract pectin and improve colour and prevent crystallisation – pectin is the essential ingredient which gives jam its setting quality. Cooking apples, currants, plums and gooseberries are high in pectin the enzyme which helps jam to set and jam made with these fruits always sets well. They are often mixed with other fruit such as strawberries or cherries which do not set so well.

Special preserving sugar may be used for jam, but cube or granulated sugar can also be used. Brown sugar does not give a good set although it does give a delicious and distinctive flavour. Honey and golden syrup are also tasty but prevent firm setting and it is advisable only to use ¼ honey or syrup to ¾ sugar if you like the flavour.

Preparing the Jam

Fruit must be cooked slowly to extract pectin, and soften skins before adding sugar, and to maintain a good colour. Once the sugar has dissolved, the mixture must be boiled rapidly without stirring, to give a higher yield, better flavour and colour. If the sugar is warmed slightly in the oven or on the side of the stove before adding, it will dissolve more quickly and speed up the cooking process. Most jams take 5-15 minutes boiling before setting point is reached. This is most easily tested by dropping a little jam on a cold plate and leaving it to cool. If the jam forms a skin and wrinkles when pushed with a finger, it is ready.

If you use a jam thermometer, boil until it reaches 220°C/105°F.

Take the jam off the heat as soon as it is ready, then stir it well before putting into warmed jars and covering. Store jam in a cool, dark place, and inspect it regularly to see that it remains in good condition.

Curds

Curds are made slightly differently from jams and do not keep for as long. They are creamy, fruit-flavoured mixtures of eggs, unsalted butter and sugar, which should be cooked in a double saucepan or in a bowl over hot water. Curds are best made in small quantities and put into small jars. They will only keep for 2 months in a cool, dry place but can be stored for longer in the freezer in suitable freezer containers. Curds are particularly delicious for tart fillings and spreads, and they can also be used as sauces for ices and puddings.

Fresh Apricot Jam

Makes about 2.25 kg/5 lb

	Metric	Imperial	American
Apricots	1.5 kg	3 lb	3 lb
Water	600 ml	1 pt	2½ cups
Butter	25 g	1 oz	2 tbsp
Sugar	1.75 kg	4 lb	8 cups

Wash the apricots and cut them in half, removing the stones. Put the fruit and water into a pan and boil for 10 minutes. Add the butter and warmed sugar and stir well to dissolve. Boil hard to setting point. Stir well put into warmed jars, seal and label.

Crofton Apricot Jam

Makes about 1.75 kg/4 lb

	Metric	Imperial	American
Dried apricots	225 g	8 oz	1⅓ cup
Water	1.2 litres	2 pts	5 cups
Apples	1 kg	2¼ lb	2¼ lb
Juice and finly grated rind of lemons	2	2	2
Sugar	1.5 kg	3 lb	6 cups
Almonds, blanched	25 g	1 oz	¼ cup

Cut the apricots in quarters and soak them in 750 ml/1¼ pts/3 cups of water for 24 hours. Peel and core the apples and cut them up. Simmer them in the remaining water until soft. Add the apricots and their soaking liquid with the lemon juice and rinds. Boil for 10 minutes. Add the warmed sugar and boil to setting point. Meanwhile, cut the almonds into strips. When the jam reaches setting point, stir in the almonds put into warmed jars, seal and label.

Ginger Apple Jam

Makes about 1.5 kg/3 lb

	Metric	Imperial	American
Apples	1 kg	2 ¼ lb	2 ¼ lb
Crystallised ginger	40 g	1½ oz	3 tbsp
Sugar	750 g	1½ lb	3 cups
Water	450 ml	¾ pt	2 cups
Juice and grated rind of lemon	1	1	1

Peel and core the apples and cut them in quarters. Mince the ginger or chop it very finely. Put layers of apple, sugar and a sprinkle of ginger in a bowl and pour on the water. Leave overnight. Put into a pan and simmer for 30 minutes. Add the lemon juice and rind, bring to the boil, and boil for 30 minutes until the fruit and syrup are transparent. Stir well put into warmed jars, seal and label.

Banana Jam

Makes about 1.5 kg/ 3lb

	Metric	Impeial	American
Bananas	450 g	1 lb	1 lb
Orange juice	900 ml	1 ½ pts	3 ¾ cups
Juice of lemon	1	1	1
Rich soft brown sugar	350 g	12 oz	1 ½ cups

Chop the bananas and put into a pan with the other ingredients. Bring to the boil and simmer gently until the bananas soften and the mixture is thick and dark, stirring frequently. Pour into warmed jars, seal and label
   This easy-to-make preserve is particularly good with plain scones.

Country Blackberry Jam

Makes about 2.75 kg/6 lb

	Metric	Imperial	American
Blackberries	1.75 kg	4 lb	4 lb
Water (optional)			
Butter	25 g	1 oz	2 tbsp
Sugar	1.75 kg	4 lb	8 cups

Wash the blackberries and put into a pan. Bring slowly to the boil, adding a few spoonfuls of water if little juice runs from the fruit. Add the butter and simmer gently until the fruit is soft. Stir in the warmed sugar and boil hard to setting point. Stir well put into warmed jars, seal and label.

Blackberry and Apple Jam

Makes about 1.5 kg/3 lb

	Metric	Imperial	American
Apples	450 g	1 lb	1 lb
Water	300 ml	½ pt	1¼ cups
Blackberries	450 g	1 lb	1 lb
Sugar	1 kg	2¼ lb	4½ cups

Peel and core the apples and cut them into pieces. Put into a pan with the water and boil to a soft purée. Add the blackberries and bring to the boil. Cook until the berries are just soft. Stir in the warmed sugar until dissolved. Boil hard to setting point. Stir well put into warmed jars, seal and label.

Traditional Blackcurrant Jam

Makes about 1.5 kg/3 lb

	Metric	Imperial	American
Blackcurrants	750 g	1½ lb	6 cups
Water	600 ml	1 pt	2½ cups
Sugar	1.5 kg	3 lb	6 cups

Strip the blackcurrants from their stems. Put into a pan with the water and boil for 10 minutes. Warm the sugar and stir it into the fruit until dissolved. Boil hard to setting point. Stir well and put into warmed jars, seal and label.

Blackcurrant Jam

Makes about 1.75 kg/4 lb

	Metric	Imperial	American
Blackcurrants	1 kg	2 ¼ lb	2 ¼ lb
Water	1.2 litres	2 pts	5 cups
Butter	25 g	1 oz	2 tbsp
Sugar	1.75 kg	4 lb	8 cups

Strip the currants from their stems and boil in the water for 10 minutes. Add the butter and warmed sugar and stir well to dissolve. Boil hard to setting point. Stir well put into warmed jars, seal and label.

Blackcurrant and Rhubarb Jam

Makes about 2.25kg/5 lb

	Metric	Imperial	American
Blackcurrants	1 kg	2 ¼ lb	2 ¼ lb
Rhubarb	350 g	12 oz	¾ lb
Water	1.2 litres	2 pts	5 cups
Butter	25 g	1 oz	2 tbsp
Sugar	1.75 kg	4 lb	8 cups

Strip the currants from their stems and put into a pan. Cut the rhubarb in small pieces and add to the currants with the water. Boil for 5 minutes. Add the butter and boil for 10 minutes. Stir in the warmed sugar to dissolve. Boil hard to setting point. Stir well put into warmed jars, seal and label.

Winter Citrus Jam

Makes about 2.25 kg/5 lb

	Metric	Imperial	American
Apples	6	6	6
Lemons	4	4	4
Bananas	6	6	6
Oranges	4	4	4
Water	4.5 litres	8 pts	20 cups
Sugar			

Peel and core the apples and cut them into pieces. Cut the lemons into thin slices and discard the pips. Peel and slice the bananas. Peel the oranges and cut the flesh into small pieces. Put the fruit and water into a pan and simmer for 2 hours. Measure the pulp and for each 600 ml/1 pt/2½ cups of pulp, allow 350 g/12 oz/1½ cups of sugar. Add the warmed sugar to the fruit, stir well and boil hard to setting point. Stir well put into warmed jars, seal and label.

Country Jam

Makes about 1.5 kg/3 lb

	Metric	Imperial	American
Raspberries	225 g	8 oz	½ lb
Redcurrants	225 g	8 oz	½ lb
Small red gooseberries	225 g	8 oz	½ lb
Rhubarb	225 g	8 oz	½ lb
Sugar	1 kg	2 ¼ lb	4 ½ cups

This is a useful jam to make at the end of the soft fruit season when there is a little of each kind of fruit left in the garden. Put the raspberries in a pan. Strip the redcurrants from their strings and add to the pan. Top and tail the gooseberries and cut the rhubarb into small pieces. Put into the pan. Simmer the fruit together until it is all soft and the juices have run out. Stir in the warmed sugar until dissolved. Boil hard to setting point. Stir well put into warmed jars, seal and label.

Date Jam

Makes about 900 g/2 lb

	Metric	Imperial	American
Dates, chopped	900 g	2 lb	5 cups
Water	600 ml	1 pt	2½ cups
Sugar	450 g	1 lb	2 cups
Juice and finly grated rind of lemon	2	2	2

Put the dates in a pan and simmer in the water for 30 minutes. Add the warmed sugar and the lemon juice and rind. Stir well until the sugar has dissolved. Boil until thick, stirring well. Put into warmed jars, seal and label.

This jam is particularly good for filling tarts and cakes.

Green Gooseberry Jam

Makes about 4.5 kg/10 lb

	Metric	Imperial	American
Gooseberries	2.75 kg	6 lb	6 lb
Water	750 ml	1¼ pts	3 cups
Butter	25 g	1 oz	2 tbsp
Sugar	2.75 kg	6 lb	12 cups

Top and tail the gooseberries and simmer in the water until soft. Add the butter and warmed sugar and stir until dissolved. Boil hard to setting point and pour into warmed jars, seal and label.

If you add a few washed fresh nettles to the jam then remove them before putting the jam in the jars, it enhances the green colour.

Marrow Jam

Makes about 2.25 kg/5 lb

	Metric	Imperial	American
Marrow	1.75 kg	4 lb	4 lb
Sugar	1.5 kg	3 lb	6 cups
Juice and finely grated rind of lemons	2	2	2
Crystallised ginger, finely chopped	100 g	4 oz	8 tbsp

Cut the marrow into small dice and put into a bowl with layers of sugar. Leave to stand in a cool place for 24 hours. Put into a preserving pan with the lemon juice and rind. Add ginger and stir well. Heat gently and stir until the sugar has completely dissolved. Bring to the boil and continue boiling for about 45 minutes until the marrow is clear and tender. Put into warmed jars, seal and label.

This is very good as a tart filling.

Add the grated rind and juice of two oranges for a sweeter jam.

Orchard Jam

Makes about 2.25 kg/5 lb

	Metric	Imperial	American
Apples	600 g	1¼ lb	1¼ lb
Seedless grapes	1.5 kg	3 lb	3 lb
Sugar	1.5 kg	3 lb	6 cups
Juice of lemon	1	1	1

Peel the apples and cut them up. Wash the grapes and remove them from their stalks. Put into the preserving pan and simmer to a pulp. Stir in the warmed sugar and lemon juice and boil hard until clear and at setting point. Pour into warmed jars, seal and label.

This is a good jam to make from windfall apples and from outdoor or greenhouse grapes which are not good enough for table use – either green or black grapes will do. We used to use it a lot for a large jam tart to serve at teatime.

Spiced Orchard Jam

Makes about 4.5 kg/10 lb

	Metric	Imperial	American
Apples	2.75 kg	6 lb	6 lb
Water	2.25 litres	4 pts	10 cups
Sugar	1.5 kg	3 lb	6 cups
Juice and grated rind of oranges	2	2	2
Raisins, finely chopped	1 kg	2 ¼ lb	2 ¼ lb
Ground cloves	5 ml	1 tsp	1 tsp
Ground cinnamon	5 ml	1 tsp	1 tsp

Peel core, and dice the apples . Boil the water and sugar and then add the orange juice and rind and the raisins. Simmer for 15 minutes. Add the apples and spices and boil for a further 15 minutes. Put into warmed jars, seal and label.

This is lovely for a tart or cake filling, and another good way of using windfall apples.

Cherry Plum Jam

Makes about 2 kg/4 ½ lb

	Metric	Imperial	American
Cherry plums	1.5 kg	3 lb	3 lb
Water	600 ml	1 pt	2½ cups
Sugar	1.5 kg	3 lb	6 cups

Cherry plums are sometimes known as 'Mirabelles', and they are small round plums not much larger then cherries. Put the plums and water into a pan and simmer until the fruit is soft. Use a slotted spoon to lift out as many stones as possible as they come to the surface. Add the warmed sugar and stir until the sugar has dissolved. Boil hard to setting point. Stir well put into warmed jars, seal and label.

Fruity Raspberry Jam

Makes about 2.75 kg/6 lb

	Metric	Imperial	American
Raspberries	2 kg	4 ½ lb	4 ½ lb
Sugar	2 kg	4 ½ lb	9 cups

Put the sugar in an ovenproof dish and place in a low oven. Bring the fruit to the boil in a preserving pan. Take off the heat and stir in the warmed sugar until it has dissolved. Put the pan back on the heat, bring to the boil and boil for just 5 minutes. Pour into warmed jars, seal and label.

This jam retains the flavour of the fruit beautifully and is very easy to make.

Country Rhubarb Jam

Makes about 1.5 kg/3 lb

	Metric	Imperial	American
Rhubarb	1 kg	2 ¼ lb	2 ¼ lb
Sugar	750 g	1½ lb	3 cups
Dates, chopped	225 g	8 oz	1¼ cups
Juice and grated rind of lemon	1	1	1

Wash the rhubarb and cut it into short lengths. Put into a pan and heat gently until the rhubarb softens. Stir in the warmed sugar, chopped dates, grated lemon juice and rind. Bring to the boil and boil hard to setting point. Stir well put into warmed jars, seal and label.

Rhubarb and Date Jam

Makes about 2.25 kg/5 lb

	Metric	Imperial	American
Rhubarb	1.5 kg	3 lb	3 lb
Dates, chopped	225 g	8 oz	1¼ cups
Butter	25 g	1 oz	2 tbsp
Sugar	1.5 kg	3 lb	6 cups

Cut the rhubarb into small pieces and put into a preserving pan with the dates and the butter. Bring to the boil, stirring well. Add the warmed sugar and stir over a low heat until the sugar has dissolved. Bring to the boil and boil hard to setting point. Stir well, pour into warmed jars, seal and label.

Old-fashioned Rhubarb and Fig Jam

Makes about 3.5 kg/8 lb

	Metric	Imperial	American
Rhubarb	1.75 kg	4 lb	4 lb
Dried figs	450 g	1 lb	3 cups
Water	45 ml	3 tbsp	3 tbsp
Root ginger	25 g	1 oz	2 tbsp
Sugar	1.75 kg	4 lb	8 cups

Cut the rhubarb into small pieces and chop the figs finely. Put the rhubarb, figs and water into a preserving pan and bring to the boil. Boil hard for 5 minutes. Crush the ginger and tie it in a piece of muslin to suspend in the pan. Add the warmed sugar and stir over a low heat until the sugar has dissolved. Boil hard to setting point. Stir well, put into warmed jars, seal and label.

This is a very traditional country jam which some people may remember from their childhood.

Rhubarb and Ginger Jam

Makes about 1.75 kg/4 lb

	Metric	Imperial	American
Rhubarb	1.5 kg	3 lb	3 lb
Sugar	1.5 kg	3 lb	6 cups
Crystallised ginger, very finely chopped	100 g	4 oz	8 tbsp

Cut the rhubarb into small pieces. Put into a bowl in layers with the sugar and leave to stand in a cool place for 24 hours. Add the ginger. Simmer gently and stir well until the sugar has dissolved. Bring to the boil and boil hard to setting point. Put into warmed jars, seal and label.

This makes a very good filling for sponge cakes.

Rose Petal and Rhubarb Jam

Makes about 750 g/1 ½ lb

	Metric	Imperial	American
Rhubarb	450 g	1 lb	1 lb
Juice of lemon	1	1	1
Sugar	450 g	1 lb	2 cups
Dark red rose petals	100 g	4 oz	¼ lb

Chop the rhubarb and put into a pan with the lemon juice and sugar. Leave to stand overnight. Cut the white tips off the rose petals then chop them and add them to the mixture. Bring to the boil and stir over a low heat until the sugar has dissolved. Boil hard to setting p"iont". Pour into warmed jars, seal and label.

This unusual jam tastes delicious with scones or crisp wholemeal biscuits.

Whole Strawberry Jam

Makes about 1.75 kg/4 lb

	Metric	Imperial	American
Small ripe strawberries	1.5 kg	3 lb	3 lb
Sugar	1.5 kg	3 lb	6 cups

Clean the strawberries and put them into a preserving pan. Stir in the sugar and leave to stand for a few hours, stirring occasionally. Heat over a low heat, stirring until the sugar dissolves then boil hard for 5 minutes. Put into warmed jars, seal and label.

Leaving the fruit and sugar to stand helps to keep the fruit whole.

You can also make this jam with a mixture of strawberries and raspberries.

Strawberry and Redcurrant Jam

Makes about 2.25 kg/5 lb

	Metric	Imperial	American
Redcurrants	1 kg	2 ¼ lb	2 ¼ lb
Water	300 ml	½ pt	1¼ cups
Small ripe strawberries	1 kg	2 ¼ lb	2 ¼ lb
Sugar	1.5 kg	3 lb	6 cups

Put the redcurrants and water into a pan and heat gently, mashing the fruit well, so that the juice runs freely. Strain the juice and put into a clean pan with the strawberries. Boil them together for 5 minutes. Add the warmed sugar and boil for a further 5 minutes to setting point. Put into warmed jars, seal and label.

The same recipe can be used, substituting raspberries for strawberries.

Strawberry and Rhubarb Jam

Makes about 2.75 kg/6 lb

	Metric	Imperial	American
Small ripe strawberries	1 kg	2 ¼ lb	2 ¼ lb
Rhubarb, finely chopped	1 kg	2 ¼ lb	2 ¼ lb
Sugar	1.75 kg	4 lb	8 cups

Put the strawberries and rhubarb into a preserving pan . Bring slowly to the boil and boil for 3 minutes. Add the warmed sugar and stir over low heat until dissolved. Bring to the boil and boil hard for 5 minutes to setting point. Stir well, pour into warmed jars, seal and label.

Tomato Jam

Makes about 3.5 kg/8 lb

	Metric	Imperial	American
Ripe tomatoes, skinned, seeded and chopped	2.75 kg	6 lb	6 lb
Juice and grated rind of lemons	6	6	6
Sugar	2.75 kg	6 lb	6 lb
Salt	5 ml	1 tsp	1 tsp
Ground ginger	15 ml	1 tbsp	1 tbsp

Put the tomatoes and lemon juice and rind into a pan and cook gently until the mixture is reduced to a pulp. Remove from the heat and gently stir in the sugar, salt and ginger. Return to a low heat and stir until the sugar has dissolved. Boil hard to setting point. Pour into warmed jars, seal and label.

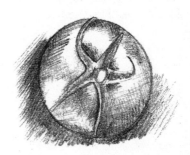

Bramble Curd

Makes about 900 g/2 lb

	Metric	Imperial	American
Blackberries	175 g	6 oz	1½ cups
Cooking apples	50 g	2 oz	½ cup
Butter	50 g	2 oz	4 tbsp
Juice and finely grated rind of lemon	1	1	1
Sugar	225 g	8 oz	1 cup
Eggs, beaten	2	2	2

Use large juicy fruit for this recipe. The curd is particularly delicious for filling tarts or for a sandwich cake when combined with a layer of whipped cream.

Put the blackberries into a pan. Peel and slice the apples and add to the berries. Simmer to a pulp and then strain through a sieve. Put this fruit purée into the top of a double saucepan or into a bowl over a pan of hot water. Add the butter, lemon juice and rind and warmed sugar. Heat until the sugar has dissolved. Add the beaten eggs and stir well until thick. Put into warmed jars, seal and label. Cool then store in the fridge.

Traditional Lemon Curd

Makes about 450 g/1 lb

	Metric	Imperial	Imperial
Butter	75 g	3 oz	6 tbsp
Sugar	225 g	8 oz	1 cup
Juice and finely grated rind of lemons	2	2	2
Eggs, beaten	2	2	2

Put the butter and sugar into the top of a double saucepan or into a bowl over a pan of boiling water. Add the lemon juice and rind. Heat and stir until the sugar has dissolved. Add the eggs and stir well over the heat until it is thick enough to coat the spoon like custard. Pour into warmed jars, seal and label. Cool then store in the fridge as it will not keep long in a store cupboard.

Lemon curd is delicious as a filling for tarts and cakes.

JELLIES

Fruit jelly is made by cooking the fruit and water together first and then straining the liquid. This juice is then boiled with sugar to give a bright, clear, firm jelly.

Apples, currants and goose-berries make particularly good jelly as they are high in pectin, and they can be mixed with other fruit to give a firm set. When fruit is being used for jelly, skins, cores and stones may be left while it is cooking, as this will add to the setting quality. The juice is strained off later to leave all the debris.

The same equipment is needed as for jam-making with the addition of a flannel jelly bag which must be suspended on a stand, or between the legs of a chair so that the juice drips into a bowl. If a jelly bag is not available, a well-boiled tea-towel can be used instead. Never squeeze the pulp to obtain more juice as this will make the jelly cloudy. Measure the juice and use 450 g/1lb/ 2 cups of sugar for each 600 ml/1pt/2½ cups of juice.

When the juice and sugar are boiled together, a little nut of butter should be added, which will prevent scum forming, and will also give brightness to the finished jelly. Test on a plate in the same way as jam, and put jelly into small jars as it is rather special.

If you sieve the fruit purée and sweeten it to

taste with a little sugar or honey, you can use it for pies or serve it with ice cream.

Blackcurrant Jelly

Makes about 900 g/2 lb

	Metric	*Imperial*	*American*
Blackcurrants	*1.5 kg*	*3 lb*	*3 lb*
Water	*600 ml*	*1 pint*	*2½ cups*
Sugar			

Wash the currants and simmer in the water for 30 minutes. Put into a jelly bag and leave the juice to drip through. Measure the juice and allow 450 g/1 lb/2 cups of sugar for each 600ml/ 1pt/ 2½ cups of juice. Warm the sugar. Bring the juice to the boil, add the warmed sugar and stir over a gentle heat until dissolved then boil hard to setting point. Pour into warmed jars, seal and label.

Country Bramble Jelly

Makes about 1.5 kg/3 lb

	Metric	Imperial	American
Blackberries	1.75 kg	4 lb	4 lb
Juice of lemons	2	2	2
Pinch of grated nutmeg			
Water	300 ml	½ pint	1¼ cups
Sugar			

Use slightly under-ripe berries and put them into a pan with the lemon juice and water. Simmer for 30 minutes until the fruit is very soft. Strain through a jelly bag and measure the juice. Allow 450 g/1 lb/2 cups of sugar for each 600 ml/1 pt/2½ cups of juice. Warm the sugar. Bring the juice to the boil, add the warmed sugar and stir over a gentle heat until dissolved then boil hard to setting point. Pour into warmed jars, seal and label.

Crabapple Jelly

Makes about 1.5 kg/3 lb

	Metric	Imperial	American
Crab apples	1.75 kg	4 lb	4 lb
Water	2.25 litres	4 pints	10 cups

Wash the fruit and cut it up without peeling or removing cores. Add the water and boil until the apples are soft. Strain through a jelly bag and measure the juice. Allow 450 g/1 lb/2 cups of sugar for each 600 ml/1 pt/2½ cups of juice. Warm the sugar. Bring the juice to the boil and stir in the warmed sugar. Stir over a gentle heat until dissolved then boil hard to setting point, pour into warmed jars, seal and label.

It is important that crabapple jelly is boiled quickly to setting point so that it keeps a bright red colour – if it is overboiled, it becomes terracotta colour.

Damson and Apple Jelly

Makes about 1.5 kg/3 lb

	Metric	Imperial	American
Damsons (or small blue plums)	1 kg	2 ¼ lb	2 ¼ lb
Apples	1 kg	2 ¼ lb	2 ¼ lb
Water			
Sugar			

Wipe the damsons and apples and cut them up without peeling, coring or stoning. Cover with water and boil for 20 minutes to a pulp. Put into a jelly bag, strain and measure the juice. Allow 450 g/1 lb/2 cups of sugar for each 600ml/1pt/2½ cups of juice. Warm the sugar. Bring the juice to the boil, stir in the warmed sugar and stir over a low heat until dissolved. Boil hard to setting point, pour into warmed jars, seal and label.

Elderberry Jelly

Makes about 1.75 kg/4 lb

	Metric	Imperial	American
Elderberries	1.75 kg	4 lb	4 lb
Apples	1 kg	2 ¼ lb	2 ¼ lb
Water			
Sugar			

Remove the elderberries from their stems and put into a pan with the apples which have been cut up without peeling or coring. Cover with water and simmer until soft and juicy. Strain through a jelly bag and measure the juice. Allow 450 ml/ 1 lb/2 cups of sugar for each 600 ml/1 pt/2½ cups of juice. Warm the sugar. Bring the juice to the boil, stir in the sugar and stir over a low heat until dissolved. Boil hard to setting point. Pour into warmed jars, seal and label.

This is a favourite North Country jelly and very cheap to make as there are always masses of elderberries in the hedgerows. We sometimes used to make it with crab apples (which were free as well), but then I liked to add the juice of two lemons when boiling the juice and sugar.

Green Gooseberry Mint Jelly

Makes about 750 g/1½ lb

	Metric	Imperial	American
Green gooseberries	1 kg	2 ¼ lb	2 ¼ lb
Water			
Sugar			
Large mint sprigs	8	8	8

Wash the fruit and cover with cold water. Boil to a pulp and then strain through a jelly bag. Measure the juice and allow 450 g/1 lb/2 cups of sugar for each 600 ml/1 pt/2½ cups of juice. Warm the sugar. Put the mint into the juice and boil for 3 minutes. Add the warmed sugar and stir over low heat until dissolved. Boil hard to setting point. Remove the mint and pour the jelly into warmed jars, seal and label.

Use as a spread or serve with roast or grilled lamb.

Lemon and Orange Jelly

Makes about 450g/1 lb

	Metric	Imperial	American
Lemons or sweet oranges	450 g	1 lb	1 lb
Water	1.2 litres	2 pints	5 cups
Sugar			

Wipe the fruit and cut it up into thin slices without peeling or removing the pips. Put into a bowl and pour over the water. Leave in a cool place to stand for 24 hours. Place in a pan and boil for 25 minutes. Leave to stand overnight and then boil again for 5 minutes. Strain through a jelly bag and measure the juice. Allow 550g/ 1¼lb/2½ cups of sugar for each 600 ml/1 pt/2½ cups of juice. Warm the sugar. Bring the juice to the boil, stir in the warmed sugar and stir over a gentle heat until dissolved. Boil hard to setting point. Pour into warmed jars, seal and label.

This is a delicious spread for breakfast toast. You can use any mixture of lemons or oranges, or just make the jelly with one type of fruit.

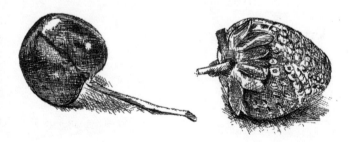

Mint Jelly

Makes about 2 kg/4 ½ lb

	Metric	Imperial	American
Apples	2.75 kg	6 lb	6 lb
Water	1.2 litres	2 pints	5 cups
Large bunch of fresh mint	1	1	1
Lemon juice	15 ml	1 tbsp	1 tbsp
Sugar			
Green vegetable colouring (optional)			

Cut up the apples without peeling or coring them and boil in the water until soft. Strain through a jelly bag and measure the juice. Allow 450 g/ 1 lb/2 cups of sugar for each 600 ml/1 pt/2½ cups of juice. Warm the sugar. Heat the juice and stir in the warmed sugar. Put half the mint into the mixture with the lemon juice and stir over a low heat until dissolved. Boil hard to setting point. Meanwhile, chop the remaining mint finely. When the jelly has reached setting point, remove the sprigs of mint. Stir in the chopped mint and a little colouring, if using, to give a bright, clear green. Put into small warmed jars, seal and label.

Serve with roast or grilled lamb.

Quince Jelly

Makes about 1.5 kg/3 lb

	Metric	Imperial	American
Quinces	1.75 kg	4 lb	4lb
Water	3 litres	5 ¼ pt	5 ¼ pt
Citric acid	10 ml	2 tsp	2tsp
sugar			

Cut the quinces into small pieces and put into a pan with 2.25 litres/4 pts/10 cups of water and the citric acid. Cover and simmer for about 1 hour until the fruit is tender. Strain through a jelly bag for 15 minutes. Remove the pulp from the bag and cook with the remaining water for 30 minutes. Strain as before and combine the juices. Add 450 g/1 lb/2 cups of sugar for each 600 ml/ 1 pt/2½ cups of juice and stir over a low heat until the sugar has dissolved. Boil hard to setting poit, pour into warmed jars, seal and label.

Raspberry and Redcurrant Jelly

Makes about 900 g/2 lb

	Metric	Imperial	American
Raspberries	750 g	1½ lb	1½ lb
Redcurrants	750 g	1½ lb	1½ lb
Water	300 ml	½ pint	1¼ cups
Sugar			

Put the fruit into a pan with the water and simmer for 15 minutes to release the juices. Strain through a jelly bag and measure the juice. Allow 450 g/1 lb/2 cups of sugar for each 600ml/ 1 pt/2½ cups of juice. Warm the sugar. Bring the juice to the boil, stir in the warmed sugar and stir over a low heat until dissolved. Boil hard to setting point. Pour into warmed jars, seal and label.

The redcurrants make this jelly set firmly and the raspberries give it a lovely flavour.

Redcurrant Jelly

Makes about 450 g/1 lb

	Metric	Imperial	American
Redcurrants	750 g	1 ½ lb	1 ½ lb
Water			
Sugar			

Wash the redcurrants and then just cover them with water. Boil for about 20 minutes until the juice is extracted. Strain through a jelly bag and measure the juice. Allow 450 g/1 lb/2 cups of sugar for each 600 ml/1 pt/2½ cups of juice. Warm the sugar. Heat the juice, stir in the sugar and stir over a low heat until dissolved. Boil hard to setting point. Pour into small warmed jars, seal and label.

Serve with lamb or game.

Rowanberry Jelly

Makes about 1.5 kg/3 lb

	Metric	Imperial	American
Apples	1.5 kg	3 lb	3 lb
Rowanberries	750 g	1 ½ lb	1 ½ lb
Water			
Sugar			

Cut up the apples without peeling or coring. Put them into a pan with the berries and cold water to cover. Boil for 25 minutes to a pulp. Strain through a jelly bag. Measure the juice and allow 450 g/1 lb/2 cups of sugar for each 600 ml/1 pt/ 2½ cups of juice. Warm the sugar. Heat the juice, stir in the warmed sugar and stir over a low heat until dissolved. Boil hard to setting point. Pour into small warmed jars, seal and label.

Serve as a spread, or as an accompaniment for cold lamb, hare or venison.

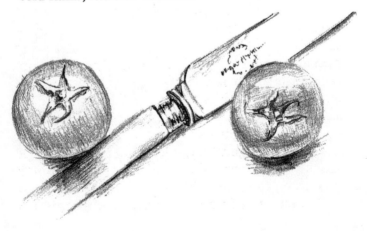

MARMALADES

These days, marmalades are usually made of citrus fruit, but the old 'marmalade' was a thick purée of fruit and sugar which set to a firm paste, so quite a lot of old recipes include apples, pears and rhubarb among the ingredients. For citrus fruit marmalade, the fruit must be sliced, simmered in water until tender, and then boiled rapidly with sugar to setting point. Some people like to soak the peel overnight, although this is not necessary, but the peel must be thoroughly soft between the fingers before sugar is added. The water in the first cooking has to be evaporated, so usually the contents of the pan are reduced to about half for a good set.

When the peel is cut, it is important to save the pips and white pith that contain pectin and help the set of the marmalade. They should be tied in a piece of muslin and hung in the preserving pan during cooking then removed before the sugar is added. The bag must be well squeezed before it is taken out to extract all the liquid.

When the sugar has been added to the hot fruit and dissolved gently, the mixture must be boiled quickly to setting point. It is ready when a little poured on to a cold plate sets and wrinkles when pushed with a finger. Always cool marmalade slightly before potting, and stir well to prevent the peel rising in the jars. Cover, seal and label in the same way as jam.

Apple Marmalade

Makes about 900 g/2 lb

	Metric	Imperial	American
Apples	1 kg	2 ¼ lb	2 ¼ lb
Chopped mixed peel	225 g	8 oz	1 ¼ cups
Water	300 ml	½ pt	1 ¼ cups
Juice of oranges	2	2	2
Sugar	750 g	1 ½ lb	3 cups

Peel and core the apples and cut them into small pieces about the size of a marble. Mince the mixed peel and simmer it in the water for 5 minutes. Add the apples and the orange juice and simmer until the apples are soft. Stir in the warmed sugar and stir over a low heat until dissolved then boil hard for 10 minutes to setting point. Stir well, pour into warmed jars, seal and label.

Cottage Marmalade

Makes about 450 g/1 lb

	Metric	Imperial	American
Rhubarb	*450 g*	*1 lb*	*1 lb*
Oranges	*3*	*3*	*3*
Sugar	*450 g*	*1 lb*	*2 cups*

Cut the rhubarb into small pieces. Grate the orange rind and add to the rhubarb. Remove the pith from the oranges and take out the pips. Tie the pith and pips in a piece of muslin. Cut the oranges in crosswise slices and cut each slice in quarters. Put the orange pieces with the rhubarb and grated rind and just cover with water. Simmer for 20 minutes until the fruit is soft and then remove the bag of pips. Stir in the warmed sugar and stir over a low heat until dissolved and then boil rapidly to setting point. Stir well and pour into warmed jars, seal and label.

Grapefruit
and Apple Marmalade

Makes about 1.5 kg/3 lb

	Metric	Imperial	American
Grapefruit	2	2	2
Water	900 ml	1 ½ pts	3 ¾ cups
Apples	750 g	1 ½ lb	1 ½ lb
Sugar	1 kg	2 ¼ lb	4 ½ cups

Cut the grapefruit in half and squeeze out the juice into a bowl. Remove the pips and scrape off the white pith from the skins. Put the pips and pith into a piece of muslin and tie on to the handle of the preserving pan. Mince the grapefruit skins and mix with the juice and water. Leave to stand overnight. Put into the pan and boil for 30 minutes. Peel and core the apples and cut them into small pieces. Add to the grapefruit mixture and cook for 15 minutes. Remove the bag of pips and pith. Stir in the warmed sugar until dissolved then boil rapidly to setting point. Stir well, pour into warmed jars, seal and label.

Pear Marmalade

Makes about 2.25 kg/5 lb

	Metric	Imperial	American
Firm pears	1.75 kg	4 lb	4 lb
Lemons	2	2	2
Oranges	3	3	3
Sugar	1.75 kg	4 lb	8 cups

Core, but do not peel the pears. Put all the fruit through the mincer. Put into the preserving pan with the sugar and stir gently over a low heat. When the sugar has dissolved, bring to the boil and boil rapidly until thick and a little sets on a plate. Pour into warmed jars, seal and label,

This is particularly good made with firm, green pears and lasts very well. You can substitute 225g/8 oz/1⅓ cups minced crystallised ginger for the oranges if you wish, stirring it in just before potting.

Orange Marmalade

Makes about 4.5 kg/10 lb

	Metric	Imperial	American
Seville oranges	1 kg	2 ¼ lb	2 ¼ lb
Lemons	2	2	2
Water	2.75 litres	5 pts	12 cups
Sugar	4.5 kg	9 lb	18 cups

Cut up the oranges and lemons into small pieces, cover with water and leave to stand overnight. Put the pips into a muslin bag and suspend in the pan. Simmer the fruit and water until the skins are soft and the contents of the pan reduced by half. Add the warmed sugar and stir over a low heat until dissolved, then boil hard to setting point. Leave to stand for 10 minutes, stir well and pour into warmed jars, seal and label.

Orange Jelly Marmalade

Makes about 2 kg/4 ½ lb

	Metric	Imperial	American
Seville oranges	1 kg	2 ¼ lb	2 ¼ lb
Water	2.5 litres	4 ½ pts	11 cups
Juice of lemons	2	2	2
Sugar	1.5 kg	3 lb	6 cups

Pare the orange rind very thinly and cut it into shreds. Put the shreds into a muslin bag and suspend over the edge of a preserving pan. Chop the fruit and add to the pan with the water and lemon juice. Bring to the boil then simmer for about 2 hours until the mixture has reduced by about one-third. Strain through a jelly bag and leave to drip. Put the juice into a clean preserving pan and stir in the sugar over a low heat until the sugar has dissolved. Remove the rind from the muslin bag, rinse under hot water then add to the pan. Boil hard to setting point skim and allow to cool. stir, pour into warmed jars, seal and label

Sweet Orange Marmalade

Makes about 2 kg/4 ½ lb

	Metric	Imperial	American
Seville oranges	8	8	8
Sweet oranges	4	4	4
Lemons	2	2	2
Water	4.5 litres	8 pts	20 cups
Sugar			

Put all the skins from the fruit through the mincer and put this pulp in the water. Leave to stand for 24 hours. Dice the fruit, taking out the pips, and put the fruit with the skins into a preserving pan. Put the pips into a muslin bag and suspend in the pan. Boil the fruit for 45 minutes, and then take out the bag of pips. Measure the pulp and allow 450 g/1 lb/2 cups of sugar for each 600 ml/1 pt/2½ cups of pulp. Warm the sugar slightly in the oven and then stir into the pulp. Stir over low heat until the sugar has completely dissolved, and then boil fast to setting point. Put into warmed jars, seal and label.

Rhubarb Marmalade

Makes about 2.75 kg/6 lb

	Metric	Imperial	American
Lemons	5	5	5
Rhubarb, chopped	1.75 kg	4 lb	4 lb
Almond essence (extract)	10 ml	2 tsp	2 tsp
Ginger essence (extract)	30 ml	2 tbsp	2 tbsp
Sugar	2.75 kg	6 lb	12 cups

Grate the rind from 3 lemons and put into a pan with 300 ml/½ pt/1¼ cups water, the juice of the lemons, the chopped rhubarb, the essences and the sugar. Stir together over low heat until the sugar has dissolved, then boil hard to setting point. Put into warmed jars, seal and label.

Keep this marmalade for a month before using. We use this as marmalade for toast, but it also makes a good tart or filling for sandwich cakes.

Green Tomato Marmalade

Makes about 2 kg/4 ½ lb

	Metric	Imperial	American
Green tomatoes	1.75 kg	4 lb	4 lb
Lemons	5	5	5
Water	150 ml	¼ pt	⅔ cup
Sugar	1 kg	2 ¼ lb	4 ½ cups

Cut up the tomatoes. Peel the lemons and cut the flesh into thin slices. Mix the tomatoes and lemons together with the water and heat slowly to the boil. Boil for 10 minutes, then stir in the sugar. Stir over low heat until the sugar has dissolved, then boil hard to setting point. Pour into warmed jars, seal and label.

A layer of this baked between two slices of bread makes a tasty tea-time snack.

Trinity Marmalade

Makes about 1.5 kg/3 lb

	Metric	Imperial	American
Grapefruit	2	2	2
Lemons	3	3	3
Oranges	3	3	3
Water			
Sugar			

Cut the fruit in half and squeeze out the juice. Put the pips into a muslin bag. Mince the peel and the pulp. Put the minced peel and pulp, juice and bag of pips into a bowl and cover with cold water, allowing 1.5 litres/2½ pts/6 cups of water for each 600 ml/1 pt/2½ cups of pulp. Leave to stand for 48 hours. Measure the mixture and allow 450 g/1 lb/2 cups of sugar for each 600 ml/ 1 pt/2½ cups of pulp. Boil the pulp for 20 minutes, then add the warmed sugar and stir well until the sugar has dissolved. Boil fast to setting point, pour into warm jars, seal and label.

I have left this to stand for as long as 5 days and it has turned out a lovely, tasty jellied preserve with no hard pieces of peel in it.

Whisky Marmalade

Makes about 3 kg/7 lb

	Metric	Imperial	American
Seville oranges	1 kg	2 ¼ lb	2 ¼ lb
Water	2.25 liters	4 pts	10 cups
Juice of lemons	2	2	2
Sugar	1.75 kg	4 lb	8 cups
Whisky	150 ml	¼ pt	⅔ cup

Halve and squeeze the oranges and removed the
pips. Chop or mince the rind finely. Tie the pips
in a muslin bag and suspend over the edge of a
preserving pan. Add the orange and lemon juice,
orange rind and water to the pan, bring to the
boil then simmer for about 2 hours until reduced
to about one-third. Remove the muslin bag, cool
slightly, then squeeze the liquid into the pan.
Add the warmed sugar and stir over a low heat
until the sugar has dissolved. Stir in the whisky.
Bring to the boil and boil hard to setting point.
Pour into warmed jars, seal and label.

BOTTLING

Fruit and tomatoes are the most successful items for bottling, vegetables, meat or poultry are not suitable for bottling at home. Successful bottling depends on heating the fruit enough, closing the jars while they are hot, and using airtight jars. Preserving jars may have glass or metal lids which rest on a rubber band, and either clips or screwbands are used to hold the lids tightly in place when the jars are cooling. When the jars are cold, the vacuum formed inside holds the lid in place. Always use clean jars and lids without ridges or chips, and be sure that rubber bands are soft and flexible if they are not attached to the lids.

Fruit should be carefully prepared for bottling and should be ripe, but not over-ripe. Unsound fruit, stalks and leaves must be removed, and the fruit rinsed in clean, cold water. Gooseberries should be topped and tailed and pricked to prevent shrivelling. Raspberries should be free from maggots, but are better not rinsed. Rhubarb needs wiping and cutting into short lengths.

Stone fruit should be just ripe and rinsed in clean, cold water. Large fruit may be halved and stoned, and peaches should be skinned. Fruit with light-coloured flesh should be covered with syrup or water as soon as possible to prevent discolouration. Hard fruit, such as apples and pears, is usually peeled, cored and cut into slices or halved, but apples may also be made into purée. Tomatoes may be bottled whole if small, or they can be cut into halves or quarters, or prepared as a purée.

Fruit may be bottled in water or syrup, but syrup keeps a better flavour and also means that fruit is ready for use without further preparation. Usually a proportion of 450 g/1 lb/2 cups of sugar to 1 litre/1¾ pints/4¼ cups of water gives a suitable strength of syrup for most fruit. Sugar and water should be boiled for 1 minute before use (either hot or cold according to method).

The two easiest bottling methods are in a slow water bath or in a moderate oven.

Slow Water Bath
Use a deep container, such as a fish kettle or preserving pan, with a false bottom so that the jars are not in direct contact with the base of the pan. Fill the bottles with fruit and cold syrup or water, and then put on the rings, lids and clips. Screw on screw-top lids then unscrew them by a quarter turn. Cover the jars in the pan with cold water and raise the temperature gradually to reach the given temperature (see next page) in 90 minutes. The water should then be maintained at that temperature for the required time (see next page), before the jars are removed from the water and the screwbands tightened and the jars left to cool.

Gooseberries for pies, pie-rhubarb and apple slices should be maintained at 85°C/185°F for 10 minutes.

Tightly packed dessert gooseberries, dessert rhubarb, whole stonefruit, apples, peaches and halved plums should be maintained at 90°C/190°F for 15 minutes.

Pears and whole tomatoes should be maintained at 95°C/195°F for 30 minutes.

Moderate Oven Method

For this oven method, put the bottles on pads of newspaper or a solid block of wood so that the glass does not touch hot metal. Preheat the oven for 15 minutes to 150°C/300°F/gas mark 2. Pack the fruit into the jars and add boiling water or syrup and adjust rings and lids. Do not put on screwbands; jars with separate screw-tops should be tightened then unscrew a quarter turn. Allow a longer time for processing for larger quantities of bottles.

For pie-gooseberries, pie-rhubarb and apple slices allow 30–40 minutes for 450 g–1.75 kg/1–4 lb (45–60 minutes for 2.25–4.5 kg/5–10 lb).

Tightly packed dessert gooseberries, dessert rhubarb and whole stone fruit need 40–50 minutes for 450 g–1.75 kg/1–4 lb (75–90 minutes for 2.25–4.5 kg/5–10 lb). Screwbands should be put on immediately the jars are taken from the oven.

When jars are quite cold, the day after

processing, the clips or screwbands should be removed and each jar carefully lifted by the lid. If it remains firm, a vacuum has formed, but if the lid comes off, the jar has not sealed properly and the fruit will not keep. In such cases, re-process the fruit or use it up immediately. The screwbands should be washed and dried thoroughly and rubbed with a little oil inside before being put on loosely for storage, but spring clips should never be stored on the bottles. Keep fruit in a cool, dry place away from sunlight, and label the jars carefully so that they are used in rotation.

PICKLES

Vinegar, sugar, salt and spices are essential for these pickles which are not difficult to make. Put the pickles into preserving jars or into screw-top jars with vinegar-proof lids. Remember paper lids will allow the vinegar to evaporate and metal lids will corrode in contact with the vinegar. Clean and sterilise the jars before use as for jam.

Use packets of pickling spice from the chemist or grocer and malt vinegar and make your own spiced vinegar by boiling the spices in the vinegar for 10 minutes before use. A ready-spiced pickling vinegar can now be bought from most supermarkets, which saves a little time. Always use cooking salt for pickling and not the free-running variety which often contains chemicals. You will find that the quantity of spiced vinegar required for the recipes will vary depending on the fruit or vegetable and the jars you use, so it is a good idea to make up the vinegar in quantity then use it as required. This also makes it easier to adjust the quantities of pickles you make.

In the summer, I make up quite a large quantity of spiced vinegar, then I can use it for any excess fruit or left over vegetables without having to take any extra trouble preparing and preserving them.

Cabbage Pickle

Makes about 2.25 kg/5 lb

	Metric	Imperial	American
Hard Cabbage	*1*	*1*	*1*
Onions	*450 g*	*1 lb*	*1 lb*
Kitchen salt	*100 g*	*4 oz*	*8 tbsp*
Vinegar	*1.5 litres*	*2.5 pts*	*6 cups*
Plain (all-purpose) flour	*50 g*	*2 oz*	*½ cup*
Sugar	*350 g*	*12 oz*	*1 ½ cups*
Curry powder	*10 ml*	*2 tsp*	*2 tsp*
Mustard powder	*30 ml*	*2 tbsp*	*2 tbsp*

Shred the cabbage and cut the onions into thin rings. Put into a bowl, sprinkle with salt and leave overnight. Drain off the salty liquid. Put into a pan with 900 ml/1½ pts/3¾ cups of vinegar and boil gently for 20 minutes. Mix the flour, sugar, curry powder, mustard and remaining vinegar. Stir into the cabbage and boil hard for 5 minutes. Put into warmed jars, seal and label .

Pickled Cherries

Makes 450 g/1 lb

	Metric	Imperial	American
Glacé (candied) cherries	*450 g*	*1 lb*	*1 lb*
Vinegar	*150 ml*	*¼ pt*	*⅔ cups*
Salt	*1.5 ml*	*¼ tsp*	*¼ tsp*
Pickling spice	*10 ml*	*2 tsp*	*2 tsp*

Fill small jars with the cherries. Put the vinegar, salt and spice into a pan and boil for 5 minutes. Strain over the cherries and cover. Be sure the cherries are really well covered in the vinegar, as they do soak it up. Keep for about 4 months before using. This recipe sounds unusual, but the pickled cherres make a particulary good accompaniment for ham or chicken.

Pickled Damsons

Makes 2.75 kg/6 lb

	Metric	Imperial	American
Damsons	2.75 kg	6 lb	6 lb
Vinegar	900 ml	1½ pts	3¾ cups
Sugar	1.75 kg	4 lb	8 cups
Pickling spice	25 g	1 oz	2 tbsp
Cloves	6	6	6

Wipe the damsons, prick them with a needle and put into a bowl. Put the vinegar and sugar into a pan and add the spice and cloves tied into a piece of muslin. Boil together for 5 minutes then pour over the fruit. Leave to stand for 24 hours. Drain off the juice, bring to the boil and pour back over the fruit. Leave to stand for a further 24 hours. Take out the spice bag, and put the fruit and juice into a pan. Bring slowly to the boil without breaking the fruit. Lift out the fruit with a slotted spoon and put into warmed jars. Boil the liquid, pour over the damsons and cover.

Fig Pickle

Makes about 900 g/2 lb

	Metric	Imperial	American
Dried figs	450 g	1 lb	1 lb
Sugar	450 g	1 lb	2 cups
Vinegar	300 ml	½ pt	1 ¼ cups
Ground cloves	5 ml	1 tsp	1 tsp
Ground mace	2.5 ml	½ tsp	½ tsp
Mustard powder	5 ml	1 tsp	1 tsp

Cover the figs with cold water and leave to soak overnight. Drain thoroughly. Put the other ingredients into a pan and heat slowly, stirring well to dissolve the sugar. Add the figs and then simmer for 1 hour. Put into small warmed jars, seal and label.

Pickled French Beans

Makes about 1.75 kg/4 lb

	Metric	Imperial	American
French beans	1.75 kg	4 lb	4 lb
Vinegar	600 ml	1 pt	2½ cups
Pickling spice	25 g	1 oz	2 tbsp
Salt	5 ml	1 tsp	1 tsp

String the beans and cut them into 2.5 cm/1 in chunks. Boil until tender in salted water. Drain and put into jars. Boil the vinegar and spice for 3 minutes and then stir in the salt. Leave until

cold and pour over the beans to cover them well.
Cover and keep for 2 months before using.

Pickled Leeks

Makes 1.75 kg/4 lb

	Metric	Imperial	American
Medium-sized leeks	1.75 kg	4 lb	4 lb
Vinegar	600 ml	1 pt	2½ cups
Pickling spice	25 g	1 oz	2 tbsp
Salt	5 ml	1 tsp	1 tsp
Sugar	5 ml	1 tsp	1 tsp

Slice the leeks across in thick slices and steam
until barely cooked, then cool and pack into small
jars. Prepare the vinegar by boiling it for 5
minutes with the spice, salt and sugar. Take out
the spices and pour the vinegar over the leeks
which you have packed into jars. Keep for two or
three weeks before using.

Mixed Pickles

Makes about 1.5 kg/3 lb

	Metric	Imperial	American
Cauliflower, French beans, Small onions, Marrow, Cucumber	1-1.5 kg	2 ¼-3 lb	2 ¼-3 lb
Vinegar	1.2 litres	2 pts	5 cups
Root ginger	15 g	½ oz	2 tbsp
Salt	15 ml	1 tbsp	1 tbsp
Water	1.2 litres	2 pts	5 cups

Use a mixture of vegetables, according to what is available, to give 1–1.5 kg/2¼–3 lb weight. Cut the cauliflower into sprigs. String the beans and cut them into small chunks. Peel and dice the onion, marrow and cucumber. Put the vinegar, spice and ginger into a pan and simmer for 20 minutes, strain and cool. Bring the salt and water to the boil and put in the prepared vegetables. Bring to the boil and simmer for 3 minutes. Drain well and put into jars. Cover with the vinegar, seal and label.

Mustard Pickles

Makes about 3.5 kg/8 lb

	Metric	Imperial	American
Onions	1.75 kg	4 lb	4 lb
Cauliflowers	3	3	3
Water	4.5 litres	8 pts	20 cups
Salt	450 g	1 lb	2 cups
Vinegar	900 ml	1½ pts	3¾ cups
Sugar	225 g	8 oz	1 cup
Mustard powder	15 ml	1 tbsp	1 tbsp
Plain (all-purpose) flour	50 g	2 oz	½ cup
Turmeric	15 ml	1 tbsp	1 tbsp

Cut the vegetables into neat small pieces. Boil the water and salt and leave until cold. Pour over the vegetables and leave to stand for 36 hours. Mix together the vinegar, sugar, mustard, flour and turmeric and bring to the boil. Drain the vegetables and add to the vinegar mixture. Bring to the boil and then simmer for 15 minutes. Pour into warmed jars, seal and label.

Some small green tomatoes, a little celery, and French beans can be added to the vegetables if liked, and a small cucumber, is good, too.

Pickled Nasturtiums

Makes 900 g/2 lb

	Metric	*Imperial*	*American*
Nasturtium seeds	*900 g*	*2 lb*	*2 lb*
Vinegar	*300 ml*	*½ pt*	*1¼ cups*
Salt	*15 ml*	*1 tbsp*	*1 tbsp*
Pickling spice	*15 ml*	*1 tbsp*	*1 tbsp*

Gather the nasturtium seeds on a dry day, when they are young and soft. Boil together the vinegar, salt and spice (tied in a bag) for 5 minutes. Put the vinegar into a preserving jar. Wipe the nasturtium seeds and drop them into the vinegar. Keep covered and add seeds from time to time and screw on the lid again. Prepare the pickle one year for use the next.

These hot, spicy seeds are used as a substitute for capers in sauce to go with lamb stew, and in fish dishes and salads. Just lift the seeds out of the jar and drain them well before use.

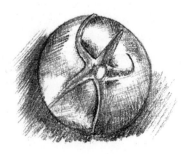

Pickled Prunes

Makes about 3 kg/7 lb

	Metric	Imperial	American
Dried prunes	3 kg	7 lb	7 lb
Vinegar	1.2 litres	2 pts	5 cups
Pickling spice	25 g	1 oz	2 tbsp

Use good quality plump prunes, wash them well and put them into small screw-top jars. Simmer the vinegar and spice for 8 minutes then remove the spice. Pour the boiling vinegar over the prunes to cover them well, and seal the jars. Leave for about 6 months before using with cold pork or ham.

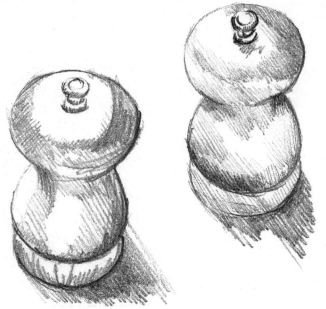

Pickled Red Cabbage

Makes about 900 g/2 lb

	Metric	Imperial	American
Red cabbage	1	1	1
Cooking salt			
Vinegar	600 ml	1 pt	2½ cups
Pickling spice	25 g	1 oz	2 tbsp
Mustard powder	5 ml	1 tsp	1 tsp

Cut the cabbage heart into four pieces and take out the centre stalk. Shred the cabbage pieces finely, put onto a large flat dish and sprinkle lightly with salt. Leave to stand for 24 hours and then drain very thoroughly. Pack into jars. Boil the vinegar, pickling spice and mustard together for 5 minutes then leave until cold. Pour over the cabbage, seal and label. Do not use the vinegar hot or it will make the cabbage blue and soft.

Pickled Onions or Shallots

Makes 3.5 kg/8 lb

	Metric	Imperial	American
Small onions or shallots.	3.5 kg	8 lb	8 lb
Salt	225 g	8 oz	1 cup
Water	2.25 litres	4 pts	10 cups
Vinegar	1.2 litres	2 pts	5 cups
Pickling spice	25 g	1 oz	2 tbsp
Sugar	10 ml	2 tsp	2 tsp

Pour boiling water over the small onions or shallots and peel them. Boil the salt and water and leave to cool. Pour over the onions then let them stand for 2 days. Drain and pack into jars. Boil the vinegar and spice for 5 minutes and leave until cold. Pour over the onions or shallots and add 1 teaspoon of sugar to each jar. Cover and leave for one month before using.

Pickled Green Walnuts

Makes 1.75 kg/4 lb

	Metric	Imperial	American
Green walnuts	1.75 kg	4 lb	4 lb
Water	600 ml	1 pt	2 ½ cups
Salt	100 g	4 oz	8 tbsp
Vinegar	600 ml	1 pt	2 ½ cups
Pickling spice	15 ml	1 tbsp	1 tbsp
Mustard powder	7.5 ml	½ tbsp	½ tbsp

Pick the walnuts in June or early July while the kernels are still very soft and the outer casings are bright green and firm. Be prepared to get your hands stained brown as walnut juice makes rather a mess. Prick the green casing of the walnuts all over with a fork. Boil the water and salt together and pour over the walnuts. Soak the walnuts in the salted water for 5 days. Drain them and put them on wooden racks spread out to turn black in the sun, turn them over often. Boil the vinegar, spice and mustard powder for 10 minutes then take out the spices. Pack the black walnuts into jars and pour over the vinegar. Cover and keep for at least two weeks before using.

CHUTNEY

Chutney is one of the nicest kitchen preserves and you can make it from all sorts of odds and ends of fruit and vegetables. Vinegar and sugar act as preservatives and dried fruit and spices add a special flavour. Do not use aluminium pans for making chutney. Do be sure to cook the chutney long enough so that it is rich and brown and as thick as jam. Pot it in clean jars and cover tightly with vinegar-proof screw-top plastic lids. Paper covers will allow the vinegar to evaporate and the chutney will become dark and dry. Store it in a cool dark place, and you will find it tastes better if kept for a few months so that the flavours have time to blend and mature.

Traditional Apple Chutney

Makes about 2 kg/4 ½ lb

	Metric	Imperial	American
Cooking apples	1 kg	2 ¼ lb	2 ¼ lb
Onions	225 g	8 oz	½ lb
Sultanas (golden raisins)	225 g	8 oz	1⅓ cups
Mustard seed	25 g	1 oz	2 tbsp
Salt	50 g	2 oz	4 tbsp
Pepper	2.5 ml	½ tsp	½ tsp
Sugar	225 g	8 oz	1 cup
Vinegar	750 ml	1 ¼ pts	3 cups
Ground ginger	15 ml	1 tbsp	1 tbsp

Peel and core the apples and cut into pieces. Peel the onions and chop them finely. Put all the ingredients into a pan and bring to the boil. Simmer until thick and brown, stirring frequently. Spoon into warmed jars, seal and label. If you do not like much ginger, only put in half the amount and taste when the chutney is finished. You can always add more if you like.

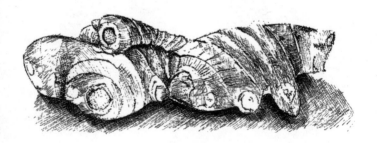

Apple Chutney

Makes about 900 g/2 lb

	Metric	Imperial	American
Cooking apples	450 g	1 lb	1 lb
Sultanas (golden raisins)	225 g	8 oz	1 ⅓ cups
Shallots or small onions	175 g	6 oz	¾ cup
Ground ginger	5 ml	1 tsp	1 tsp
Sugar	200 g	7 oz	¾ –1 cup
Salt	15 ml	1 tbsp	1 tbsp
Vinegar	600 ml	1 pt	2½ cups

Peel and core the apples and chop them finely.
Mix with the sultanas. Peel and chop the shallots
or onions finely. Mix all the ingredients together
and leave to stand for 1 hour. Place all the
ingredients in a pan. Simmer until thick and
brown, stirring often to prevent burning. Spoon
into warmed jars, cover, seal and label.

Apple and Red Tomato Chutney

Makes about 4 kg/9 lb

	Metric	Imperial	American
Cooking apples	1.5 kg	3 lb	3 lb
Red tomatoes	1.5 kg	3 lb	3 lb
Onions	450 g	1 lb	1 lb
Sugar	450 g	1 lb	2 cups
Ground ginger	5 ml	1 tsp	1 tsp
Vinegar	1.2 litres	2 pts	5 cups
Salt	50 g	2 oz	4 tbsp
Pickling spice	25 g	1 oz	2 tbsp

Peel and cut up the apples, tomatoes and onions and put them into a pan with the sugar and ginger. In a separate pan, put the vinegar and salt . Tie the pickling spice into a muslin bag and add to the vinegar. Bring to the boil and boil for 3 minutes. Take out the spice bag. Pour the vinegar over the other ingredients and simmer until thick and brown, stirring well. Spoon into warmed jars, seal and label.

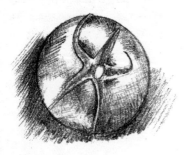

Newton Apple Chutney

Makes about 5 kg/11 lb

	Metric	Imperial	American
Apples	2 kg	4 ½ lb	4 ½ lb
Ripe tomatoes	450 g	1 lb	1 lb
Onions	450 g	1 lb	1 lb
Sultanas (golden raisins)	450 g	1 lb	2 ⅔ cups
Vinegar	1.75 litres	3 pts	7 ½ cups
Golden (light corn) syrup	900 g	2 lb	3 cups
Salt	20 ml	4 tsp	4 tsp
Mustard powder	5 ml	1 tsp	1 tsp
Ground ginger	15 ml	1 tbsp	1 tbsp
Juice and grated rind of lemons	2	2	2

Peel, core and cut up the apples. Peel and cut up the tomatoes. Peel the onions and chop them finely. Put the apples, tomatoes and onions into a pan with the vinegar and boil until the onions are soft. Add the syrup, salt, mustard, ginger and grated rind and juice of the lemons. Boil until thick and brown. Spoon into warmed jars, seal and label.

This is a mild and useful chutney which is delicious with any kind of meat. It can also be heated to serve as a good apple sauce with pork or sausages.

Mixed Autumn Chutney

Makes about 3.5 kg/8 lb

	Metric	Imperial	American
Pears	1 kg	2 ¼ lb	2 ¼ lb
Apples	1 kg	2 ¼ lb	2 ¼ lb
Onions	450 g	1 lb	1 lb
Dates	450 g	1 lb	2 ⅔ cups
Vinegar	1.2 litres	2 pts	5 cups
Pickling spice	30 ml	2 tbsp	2 tbsp
Salt	30 ml	2 tbsp	2 tbsp
Mustard powder	30 ml	2 tbsp	2 tbsp
Ground ginger	30 ml	2 tbsp	2 tbsp
Golden (light corn) syrup	1 kg	2 ¼ lb	2 ⅔ cups

Peel and core the pears and apples and cut them into small pieces. Peel and chop the onions, and chop the dates. Put the vinegar into a pan with the pickling spice tied in a bag. Add the salt, mustard, ginger and syrup and boil together for 5 minutes. Remove the spice bag. Put in the pears, apples, onions and dates and simmer together until thick and brown, stirring frequently. Spoon into warmed jars, seal and label.

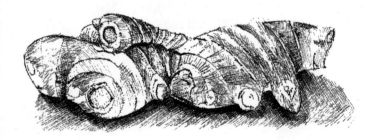

Banana Chutney

Makes about 4 kg/9 lb

	Metric	Imperial	American
Bananas	16	16	16
Onions, finely chopped	1 kg	2 ¼ lb	2 ¼ lb
Dates, finely chopped	450 g	1 lb	2 ½ cups
Crystallised ginger	225 g	8 oz	1 ⅓ cups
Salt	15 ml	1 tbsp	1 tbsp
Pickling spice	25 g	1 oz	2 tbsp
Vinegar	1.2 litres	2 pts	5 cups
Sugar	450 g	1 lb	2 cups

Peel and slice the bananas and put them into a pan. Add the onions, dates, ginger and salt. Put the pickling spice into a bag and hang in the pan. Add the vinegar, bring to the boil and boil for 5 minutes. Take out the spice bag. Stir in the sugar and simmer over low heat until rich and brown, stirring frequently. Spoon into warmed jars, seal and label.

75

Bishopton Chutney

Makes about 2 kg/4 ½ lb

	Metric	Imperial	American
Cooking apples	1 kg	2 ¼ lb	2 ¼ lb
Raisins, chopped	450 g	1 lb	2 ⅔ cups
Garlic, thinly sliced	100 g	4 oz	¼ lb
Sugar	450 g	1 lb	2 cups
Vinegar	600 ml	1 pt	2½ cups
Salt	5 ml	1 tsp	1 tsp
Ground ginger	2.5 ml	½ tsp	½ tsp
Pinch of pepper			

Peel and chop the apples finely. Add the raisins and garlic. Stir in the remaining ingredients. Bring to the boil, stirring well, and then simmer until brown and thick. Spoon into warmed jars, seal and label.

No-cook Date Chutney

Makes about 1.75 kg/4 lb

	Metric	Imperial	American
Pickling spice	25 g	1 oz	2 tbsp
Vinegar	600 ml	1 pt	2½ cups
Dates, minced	900 g	2 lb	2 lb
Crystallised ginger, minced	450 g	1 lb	1 lb
Mustard powder	10 ml	2 tsp	2 tsp
Golden (light corn) syrup	90 ml	6 tbsp	6 tbsp

Put the spice into a muslin bag and add to the vinegar in a pan. Boil together for 7 minutes. Add the dates and ginger, mustard and syrup and stir thoroughly. Leave to stand until cool and stir again. Spoon into warmed jars, seal and label.

Mixed Fruit Chutney

Makes about 2.25 kg/5 lb

	Metric	Imperial	American
Cooking apples	1.5 kg	3 lb	3 lb
Large onions	3	3	3
Large tomatoes	4	4	4
Sultanas (golden raisins)	350 g	12 oz	2 cups
Soy sauce	15 ml	1 tbsp	1 tbsp
Salad oil	30 ml	2 tbsp	2 tbsp
Salt	15 ml	1 tbsp	1 tbsp
Ground ginger	5 ml	1 tsp	1 tsp
Anchovy essence (extract)	5 ml	1 tsp	1 tsp
Pepper	5 ml	1 tsp	1 tsp
Mustard seed	5 ml	1 tsp	1 tsp
Vinegar	300 ml	½ pt	1¼ cups

Peel, core and chop the apples finely. Peel and chop the onions and tomatoes. Put all the ingredients into a pan and simmer very gently until thick and brown. Spoon into warmed jars, seal and label.

Gooseberry Chutney

Makes about 4 kg/9 lb

	Metric	Imperial	American
Green gooseberries	1 kg	2 ¼ lb	2 ¼ lb
Mixed candied peel	225 g	8 oz	1 ⅓ cups
Sultanas (golden raisins)	450 g	1 lb	2 ⅔ cups
Garlic, chopped	25 g	1 oz	2 tbsp
Salt	100 g	4 oz	8 tbsp
Sugar	450 g	1 lb	2 cups
Pepper	5 ml	1 tsp	1 tsp
Crystallised ginger, chopped	50 g	2 oz	⅓ cup
Curry powder	50 g	2 oz	⅓ cup
Onions, finely chopped	450 g	1 lb	1 lb
Vinegar	1.2 litres	2 pts	5 cups

Top and tail the gooseberries and put them into a pan. Add the chopped peel and sultanas. Stir in chopped garlic, salt, sugar, pepper, ginger and curry powder. Stir in the onions. Bring to the boil, stirring well, then simmer until brown and thick. Spoon into warmed jars, seal and label.

Marrow Chutney

Makes about 2 kg/4 ½ lb

	Metric	Imperial	American
Large marrow	1	1	1
Cooking salt	30 ml	2 tbsp	2 tbsp
Vinegar	1.2 litres	2 pts	5 cups
Mustard powder	15 ml	1 tbsp	1 tbsp
Turmeric	30 ml	2 tbsp	2 tbsp
Ground ginger	30 ml	2 tbsp	2 tbsp
Sugar	100 g	4 oz	½ cup
Large onions, finely chopped	2	2	2

Peel and dice the marrow. Weigh out 1.5 kg/3 lb of marrow. Sprinkle with the salt and leave to stand for 24 hours.

Drain off the liquid and put the marrow into a pan. Mix together the vinegar, mustard, turmeric, ginger and sugar and add to the pan. Add the onions. Bring to the boil and then simmer until thick and brown, stirring frequently. Spoon into warmed jars, seal and label.

Orange Chutney

Makes about 4.5 kg/10 lb

	Metric	Imperial	American
Cooking apples	1.5 kg	3 lb	3 lb
Peeled oranges	225 g	8 oz	½ lb
Dates, minced	750 g	1 ½ lb	1 ½ lb
Red tomatoes, sliced	750 g	1 ½ lb	1 ½ lb
Sugar	1.5 kg	3 lb	6 cups
Vinegar	3.4 litres	6 pts	12 cups
Chillies	50 g	2 oz	½ cup
Salt	15 ml	1 tbsp	1 tbsp

Peel, core and chop the apples and mix with the diced oranges (don't use the orange peel). Add the dates and tomatoes. Add the sugar, vinegar, chopped chillies and salt and bring to the boil. Simmer until thick and brown, stirring frequently. Spoon into warmed jars, seal and label.

The chillies make this a hot chutney, and may be omitted. A little ground ginger may be added instead.

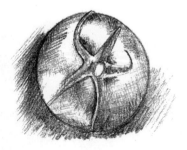

Peggy's Pear Chutney

Makes about 3.5 kg/8 lb

	Metric	Imperial	American
Pears	2 kg	4 ½ lb	4 ½ lb
Onions	450 g	1 lb	1 lb
Salt	30 ml	2 tbsp	2 tbsp
Sugar	750 g	1 ½ lb	3 cups
Ground ginger	15 ml	1 tbsp	1 tbsp
Dates, chopped	450 g	1 lb	1 lb
Sultanas (golden raisins)	225 g	8 oz	1 ⅓ cups
Mustard powder	15 ml	1 tbsp	1 tbsp
Vinegar	1.2 litres	2 pts	5 cups

Peel, core and chop the pears. Peel the onions and chop them finely. Put the onions and pears into a pan with the salt, sugar, ginger, chopped dates, sultanas, mustard and vinegar. Bring to the boil and then simmer until thick and brown, stirring frequently. Spoon into warmed jars, seal and label.

Boiling time will depend on the ripeness of the pears.

Green Plum Chutney

Makes about 3 kg/7 lb

	Metric	Imperial	American
Stoned unripe plums	2 kg	4 ½ lb	4 ½ lb
Large onions	2	2	2
Raisins	450 g	1 lb	2 ⅔ cups
Sugar	450 g	1 lb	2 cups
Cooking apples, chopped	450 g	1 lb	1 lb
Salt	15 ml	1 tbsp	1 tbsp
Pepper	5 ml	1 tsp	1 tsp
Ground ginger	15 g	½ oz	1 tbsp
Mustard seed	15 g	½ oz	1 tbsp
Vinegar	600 ml	1 pt	2 ½ cups
Pickling spice	25 g	1 oz	2 tbsp

Use green unripe plums and stone them before weighing. Cut up the plums and chop the onions finely. Place in a pan and mix with the raisins, sugar, chopped apples, salt, pepper, ginger and mustard. Tie the spice in a muslin bag and boil in the vinegar for 6 minutes remove the spice. Pour the spiced vinegar over the other ingredients and simmer gently until brown and thick. Spoon into warmed jars, seal and label.

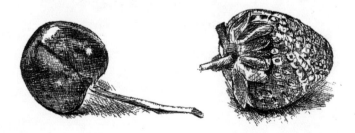

Muscovado Rhubarb Chutney

Makes about 2.25 kg/5 lb

	Metric	Imperial	American
Rhubarb	1 kg	2 ¼ lb	2 ¼ lb
Sultanas, (golden raisins)	450 g	1 lb	2 ⅔ cups
Muscovado sugar	1 kg	2 ¼ lb	2 ¼ lb
Large onion, chopped	1	1	1
Salt	30 ml	2 tbsp	2 tbsp
Ground ginger	30 ml	2 tbsp	2 tbsp
Pepper	2.5 ml	½ tsp	½ tsp
Lemons	2	2	2
Vinegar	600 ml	1 pt	2½ cups

Cut the rhubarb into small pieces. Put into a pan
with the sultanas, sugar and chopped onion. Add
the salt, ginger and pepper. Peel the lemons and
remove the pips. Cut the lemon flesh into small
pieces and add to the other ingredients. Pour in
the vinegar and bring to the boil. Stir well and
simmer until brown and thick, stirring
frequently. Spoon into warmed jars, seal and
label.

Rhubarb Chutney

Makes about 2 kg/4 ½ lb

	Metric	Imperial	American
Rhubarb	750 g	1½ lb	1½ lb
Onions	750 g	1½ lb	1½ lb
Garlic	100 g	4 oz	¼ lb
Vinegar	600 ml	1 pt	2½ cups
Sugar	450 g	1 lb	2 cups
Salt	5 ml	1 tsp	1 tsp
Pepper	2.5 ml	½ tsp	½ tsp
Ground cloves	2.5 ml	½ tsp	½ tsp

Cut the rhubarb, onions and garlic into small pieces. Add the vinegar and boil for 15 minutes. Add the remaining ingredients and simmer for about 1 hour until thick and brown, stirring freqently. Spoon into warmed jars, seal and label.

Thornton-le-Dale Chutney

Makes about 4.5 kg/10 lb

	Metric	Imperial	American
Apples	2 kg	4 ½ lb	4 ½ lb
Ripe tomatoes	1 kg	2 ¼ lb	2 ¼ lb
Onions	1 kg	2 ¼ lb	2 ¼ lb
Sugar	750 g	1 ½ lb	3 cups
Salt	30 ml	2 tbsp	2 tbsp
Pepper	30 ml	2 tbsp	2 tbsp
Ground ginger	30 ml	2 tbsp	2 tbsp
Mustard seed	15 ml	1 tbsp	1 tbsp
Raisins	450 g	1 lb	2 ⅔ cups
Vinegar	1.2 litres	2 pts	5 cups

Peel the apples, tomatoes and onions and mince
them all together. Place in a pan and add all the
other ingredients. Simmer until thick and brown,
stirring frequently. Spoon into warmed jars, seal
and label.

Green Tomato Chutney

Makes about 4.5 kg/10 lb

	Metric	Imperial	American
Green tomatoes	2 kg	4 ½ lb	4 ½ lb
Cooking apples	1 kg	2 ¼ lb	2 ¼ lb
Shallots or small onions	450 g	1 lb	1 lb
Dates	450 g	1 lb	1 lb
Vinegar	1.75 litres	3 pts	7 ½ cups
Golden (light corn) syrup	1 kg	2 ¼ lb	2 ¼ lb
Mustard powder	7.5 ml	½ tbsp	½ tbsp
Salt	45 ml	3 tbsp	3 tbsp
Pepper	10 ml	2 tsp	2 tsp

Cut the tomatoes into small pieces without peeling. Peel and core the apples and cut them into pieces. Peel and chop the shallots or onions, and chop the dates. Put the shallots or onions into a pan with the vinegar and simmer until they are soft. Add the remaining ingredients and simmer for about 1 hour until thick and brown, stirring frequently. Spoon into warmed jars, seal and label.

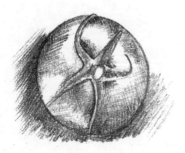

Red Tomato Chutney

Makes about 1.75 kg/4 lb

	Metric	Imperial	American
Ripe tomatoes	450 g	1 lb	1 lb
Cooking apples	450 g	1 lb	1 lb
Onions	225 g	8 oz	½ lb
Sultanas (golden raisins)	225 g	8 oz	1 ⅓ cups
Crystallised ginger	225 g	8 oz	½ lb
Chillies	12	12	12
Salt	5 ml	1 tsp	1 tsp
Sugar	225 g	8 oz	1 cup
Vinegar	600 ml	1 pt	2 ½ cups

Peel the tomatoes, apples and onions and mince them with the sultanas, ginger and chillies. Put all the ingredients into a pan, bring to the boil and then simmer until thick and brown, stirring frequently. Spoon into warmed jars, seal and label.

The chillies make this chutney quite hot, so omit them if you like.

Tomato and Onion Chutney

Makes about 2.75 kg/6 lb

	Metric	Imperial	American
Ripe tomatoes	1.5 kg	3 lb	3 lb
Onions	450 g	1 lb	1 lb
Salt	25 ml	1½ tbsp	1½ tbsp
Vinegar	1.2 litres	2 pts	5 cups
Sugar	450 g	1 lb	2 cups
Mustard powder	30 ml	2 tbsp	2 tbsp
Pickling spice	30 ml	2 tbsp	2 tbsp

Peel and slice the tomatoes and onions. Sprinkle with salt and leave to stand overnight. Place tomatoes and onions in a pan add the vinegar, sugar and mustard and bring to the boil. Put the spice into a muslin bag and hang it in the pan. After the mixture has boiled for 5 minutes, take out the spice bag. Continue simmering until the chutney is thick and brown, stirring frequently. Spoon into warmed jars, seal and label.

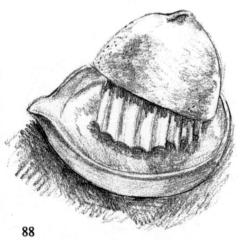

DRESSINGS, SAUCES AND KETCHUPS

I like to make a lot of different sauces and ketchups to use in the winter months; quite often I just sieve my chutney mixtures and bottle those. It is best to put sauces into sterilised sauce bottles with screw-top vinegar-proof lids, and then the bottles should be heated in a sterilised water bath in the same way as bottled fruit (see page 53). These days, it's quite a good idea to freeze the fruit sauces in small containers, which saves the bother of sterilising them.

Apple Sauce

Makes about 3 kg/7 lb

	Metric	Imperial	American
Apples	2 kg	4 ½ lb	4 ½ lb
Vinegar	1.2 litres	2 pts	5 cups
Onions, finely chopped	225 g	8 oz	½ lb
Dates, chopped	225 g	8 oz	½ lb
Salt	30 ml	2 tbsp	2 tbsp
Ground ginger	30 ml	2 tbsp	2 tbsp
Golden (light corn) syrup	1 kg	2 ¼ lb	2 ¼ lb

Cut the apples into small pices without peeling them. Put into a pan with the vinegar, onions, dates, salt and ginger. Simmer until the apples and onions are soft and then stir in the golden syrup. Continue cooking until the mixture is thick and then put through a sieve. Reheat, put into bottles or preserving jars, seal and sterilise.

This is very good served with sausages, bacon or pork.

Banana Sauce

Makes about 1.75 kg/4 lb

	Metric	Imperial	American
Bananas	10	10	10
Onions	450 g	1 lb	1 lb
Dates	450 g	1 lb	1 lb
Golden (light corn) syrup	450 g	1 lb	1 lb
Salt	15 ml	1 tbsp	1 tbsp
Ground ginger	30 ml	2 tbsp	2 tbsp
Turmeric	15 ml	1 tbsp	1 tbsp
Vinegar	900 ml	1½ pts	3¾ cups

Peel and mash the bananas. Mince the onions and dates together and add to the bananas. Stir in the remaining ingredients and bring to the boil. Simmer until thick and brown and then put through a sieve. Reheat, put into bottles or preserving jars, seal and sterilise.

Bramble Ketchup

Makes about 1.75 kg/4 lb

	Metric	Imperial	American
Ripe blackberries	2 kg	4 ½ lb	4 ½ lb
Sugar	1 kg	2 ¼ lb	4 ½ cups
Vinegar	600 ml	1 pt	2 ½ cups
Ground cloves	10 ml	2 tsp	2 tsp
Ground cinnamon	10 ml	2 tsp	2 tsp
Ground allspice	5 ml	1 tsp	1 tsp

Put all the ingredients into a pan and bring to the boil. Simmer until thick and put through a sieve. Reheat, put into bottles or preserving jars, seal and sterilise.

Date Sauce

Makes about 900 g/2 lb

	Metric	Imperial	American
Dates	450 g	1 lb	1 lb
Sultanas (golden raisins)	100 g	4 oz	⅔ cup
Onions	100 g	4 oz	¼ lb
Golden (light corn) syrup	100 g	4 oz	⅓ cup
Salt	5 ml	1 tsp	1 tsp
Ground ginger	5 ml	1 tsp	1 tsp
Pepper	1.5 ml	¼ tsp	¼ tsp
Vinegar	600 ml	1 pt	2 ½ cups

Mince the dates, sultanas and onions. Put into a pan with all the other ingredients and bring to the boil. Simmer until thick and put through a sieve. Reheat, put into bottles or preserving jars, seal and sterilise.

Farmhouse Sauce

Makes about 900 ml/1 ½ pts/3 ¾ cups

	Metric	Imperial	American
Vinegar	*1.2 litres*	*2 pts*	*5 cups*
Salt	*15 ml*	*1 tbsp*	*1 tbsp*
Garlic, chopped	*15 ml*	*1 tbsp*	*1 tbsp*
Pepper	*15 ml*	*1 tbsp*	*1 tbsp*
Ground cloves	*15 ml*	*1 tbsp*	*1 tbsp*
A little black treacle (molasses)			

Simmer all the ingredients for 20 minutes, and sweeten to taste with the treacle. Strain and put into bottles. This sauce is ideal with tomato juice and to season steaks.

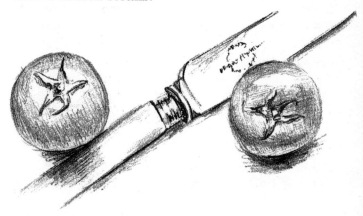

Plum Sauce

Makes about 1.75 kg/4 lb

	Metric	Imperial	American
Ripe plums	1.5 kg	3 lb	3 lb
Golden (light corn) syrup	750 g	1 ½ lb	2 cups
Vinegar	900 ml	1 ½ pts	3¾ cups
Ground ginger	15 ml	1 tbsp	1 tbsp
Salt	15 ml	1 tbsp	1 tbsp
Pepper	2.5 ml	½ tsp	½ tsp
Ground cloves	15 ml	1 tbsp	1 tbsp

Put all the ingredients together in a pan and bring to the boil. Simmer for 1 hour. Put through a sieve. Reheat, put into bottles or preserving jars, seal and sterilise.

Tomato Sauce

Makes about 3 kg/7 lb

	Metric	Imperial	American
Ripe tomatoes	2.75 kg	6 lb	6 lb
Onions	1 kg	2 ¼ lb	2 ¼ lb
Salt	60 ml	4 tbsp	4 tbsp
Pepper	2.5 ml	½ tsp	½ tsp
Mustard	30 ml	2 tbsp	2 tbsp
Golden (light corn) syrup	1 kg	2 ¼ lb	2 ¼ lb
Vinegar	600 ml	1 pt	2 ½ cups

Peel the tomatoes and cut them in half. Peel and slice the onions. Put into separate bowls and sprinkle both with the salt. Leave to stand overnight.

Drain and put into a pan with all the other ingredients. Bring to the boil and then simmer for 1¼ hours. Put through a sieve. Reheat, put into bottles or preserving jars, seal and sterilise.

Horseradish Sauce
(Non-keeping)

Makes about 60 ml/4 tbsp

	Metric	Imperial	American
Sweetened condensed milk	30 ml	2 tbsp	2 tbsp
Salt	5 ml	1 tsp	1 tsp
Vinegar	30 ml	2 tbsp	2 tbsp
Finely grated horseradish	30 ml	2 tbsp	2 tbsp

Stir the salt into the milk and gradually drip in the vinegar, stirring all the time. When smooth and thick, mix in the horseradish.

This sauce is an ideal accompaniment for beef or smoked fish.

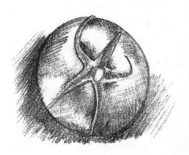

Condensed Milk Salad Dressing
(Non-keeping)

Makes about 60 ml/4 tbsp

	Metric	Imperial	American
Sweetened condensed milk	30 ml	2 tbsp	2 tbsp
Vinegar	30 ml	2 tbsp	2 tbsp
Made mustard	2.5 ml	½ tsp	½ tsp
Pepper	1.5 ml	¼ tsp	¼ tsp
Salt	2.5 ml	½ tsp	½ tsp

Put the milk into a bowl and drip in the vinegar, stirring all the time and at the same time add in the seasonings. If you like a sharp dressing include a little more vinegar.

Mustard Dressing
(Non-Keeping)

Makes about 450 ml/¾ pt/2 cups

	Metric	Imperial	American
Made mustard	15 ml	1 tbsp	1 tbsp
Sugar	15 ml	1 tbsp	1 tbsp
Cornflour (cornstarch)	15 ml	1 tbsp	1 tbsp
Pinch of pepper			
Salt	5 ml	1 tsp	1 tsp
Celery seed	5 ml	1 tsp	1 tsp
Vinegar	600 ml	1pt	2½ cups

Mix together the mustard, sugar, cornflour, pepper, salt and celery seed. Stir in the vinegar and put into a double saucepan, or a bowl over hot water. Cook until thickened and pour into a preserving jar. Keep covered in the refrigerator.

This is delicious served with beef or with fish.

Darlington Salad Cream
(Non-keeping)

Makes about 90 ml/6 tbsp

	Metric	Imperial	American
Salt	5 ml	1 tsp	1 tsp
Sugar	5 ml	1 tsp	1 tsp
Made mustard	5 ml	1 tsp	1 tsp
Cornflour (cornstarch)	15 ml	1 tbsp	1 tbsp
Egg	1	1	1
Milk	150 ml	¼ pt	⅔ cup
Melted butter or margarine	30 ml	2 tbsp	2 tbsp
Vinegar	65 ml	2 ½ fl oz	4 ½ tbsp

Put the salt, sugar, mustard, cornflour, egg and milk into a pan and heat slowly, stirring well. Add the melted fat and gradually stir in the vinegar. Cook over very gentle heat until thick and creamy.

PASTES AND BUTTERS

The pastes and butters in this chapter are easy to prepare and make quick tea-time snacks

Chicken Paste

Makes about 750 g/1 ½ lb

	Metric	Imperial	American
Cooked chicken	450 g	1 lb	1 lb
Cooked bacon	175 g	6 oz	⅜ lb
Salt and pepper			
Softened butter	75 g	3 oz	⅓ cup

Use all the odd bits of dark and light meat from the chicken, and pieces of a bacon joint. Mince the chicken and bacon together through a fine grinder. Mash with seasoning to taste and with softened butter. Pack into small jars and store in the fridge.

This is very good served at teatime on bread, toast or biscuits, or used in sandwiches.

Potted Beef

Makes about 900 g/2 lb

	Metric	Imperial	American
Butter	225 g	8 oz	1 cup
Rump steak	750 g	1 ½ lb	1 ½ lb
Salt and pepper			

Put half the butter into a casserole. Add the steak cut into small pieces, and season with salt and pepper. Cover and put the casserole into a pan of hot water. Simmer for 3 hours until the beef is completely tender (no water must get into the beef). Mince the beef and mix with the liquid which has run out, and with the remaining butter. Adjust seasoning to taste. Put into small jars and cool. Cover with extra melted butter if you want to keep it longer.

This is a very special teatime spread or it can be used for sandwiches.

Peanut Butter

Makes about 450 g/1 lb

	Metric	Imperial	American
Peanuts	450 g	1 lb	1 lb
Salt	2.5 ml	½ tsp	½ tsp
Olive oil	15 ml	1 tbsp	1 tbsp

Put shelled peanuts into a moderate oven and heat until the pink skins will come off. Rub off the skins and mince the nuts twice to get them very fine. Add salt and oil and mix thoroughly. Put into a dish in the oven at 150°C/300°F/gas mark 2 for 15 minutes. Stir well to prevent burning. Cool and put into a screw-top jar.

This makes a very good sandwich filling on its own or with some grated cheese.

Cheese Spread

Makes about 100 g/4 oz

	Metric	Imperial	American
Grated cheese	100 g	4 oz	1 cup
Butter	25 g	1 oz	2 tbsp
Salt	2.5 ml	½ tsp	½ tsp
Mustard powder	2.5 ml	½ tsp	½ tsp
Egg	1	1	1
Pinch of pepper			

Grate the cheese finely. Cream the butter, salt, mustard, egg and pepper and work in the cheese.

Put into small pots and keep in a cold place – top with melted butter if you like.

This is tasty spread on toast and grilled until bubbling. It can be used for sandwiches, or spread on bread instead of butter when making meat sandwiches to enhance the filling.

Rum Butter

Makes about 750 g/1 ½ lb

	Metric	Imperial	American
Nutmeg	½	½	½
Soft brown sugar	450 g	1 lb	2 cups
Butter	225 g	8 oz	1 cup
Rum	75 ml	5 tbsp	5 tbsp

Grate the nutmeg into the sugar. Soften the butter and whip it into the sugar with the rum until it is soft and creamy. You can add a little more rum if you prefer a strong taste. Put it in a glass dish to set.

Apple and Plum 'Butter'

Makes about 2 kg/4 ½ lb

	Metric	Imperial	American
Apples	1.5 kg	3 lb	3 lb
Plums, stoned	450 g	1 lb	1 lb
Sugar			

Peel and core the apples and cut into slices. Cook in a very little water until soft. Add the plums and cook until soft. Rub through a sieve measure the pulp. Stir in 350 g/12 oz/1½ cups of sugar to each 600 ml/1 pt/2½ cups of pulp. Bring to the boil and boil hard to setting point.

This is a stiff preserve which can be used with bread and butter or sliced and eaten as a dessert with cream.

Cherry 'Butter'

Makes about 1.5 kg/3 lb

	Metric	Imperial	American
Cherries, stoned	2 kg	4 lb	4 lb
Grated rind and juice of lemon	1	1	1
Sugar	1 kg	2 ¼ lb	4 ½ cups

Blanch and skin the cherries. Arrange them in a bowl, layering with the sugar and lemon juice. Leave overnight.

Place in a pan and bring to the boil. Boil hard for 20 minutes until very thick, stirring frequently. Spoon into warmed jars, seal and label.

This perserve will keep for about 6 weeks.

SYRUPS AND MINERALS

Home-made drinks can be enjoyed by all the family. The fruit syrups make delicious summer drinks or soothing night caps. Fruit vinegars are easy to prepare and make unusual sauces for puddings.

Dandelion Beer

Makes about 9 litres/2 gallons

	Metric	Imperial	American
Green dandelion leaves	75 g	3 oz	1 cup
Hops	50 g	2 oz	½ cup
Liquorice	15 ml	1 tbsp	1 tbsp
Root ginger	15 ml	1 tbsp	1 tbsp
Sugar	1.5 kg	3 lb	6 cups
Fresh yeast	15 g	½ oz	1 tbsp

Put the dandelion leaves, hops, liquorice and bruised ginger into a muslin bag. Put into a pan with 14 litres/24½ pts/59½ cups water. Boil for 30 minutes and then discard the muslin bag. Stir the sugar into the hot liquid until dissolved. Leave until lukewarm and then stir in the yeast. Leave to stand overnight and put into screwtop beer or cider bottles.

This will be ready for use in 2 days and is an ideal drink for the family in summer time.

Elderberry Syrup

Makes about 1.2 litres/2 pts/ 5 cups

	Metric	Imperial	American
Water	1.2 litres	2 pts	5 cups
Elderberries	1 kg	2 ¼ lb	2 ¼ lb
Root ginger	1 piece	1 piece	1 piece
Cloves	6	6	6
Sugar			

Put the water, berries, ginger and cloves into a pan and simmer for 30 minutes. Strain and measure the liquid. Allow 225 g/8 oz/1 cup of sugar to each 600 ml/1 pt/2½ cups of liquid. Boil together for 10 minutes, pour into bottles, seal and sterilise as for bottled fruit. Syrup can also be frozen in polythene containers.

Use a little in cold water for a summer drink, or with boiling water as a nightcap for a cold. Some people add 1 tablespoon gin to each 600 ml/1 pt/2½ cups syrup.

Fruit Syrup

Use any ripe soft fruit to make syrup. You can use raspberries and redcurrants together, strawberries, blackcurrants, blackberries, peaches, apricots or plums, which all make good syrups.

Put any quantity into an earthenware casserole with 150 ml/¼ pt/⅔ cup of water. Cover with a lid and leave in the oven at 150°C/300°F/Gas Mark 2 for 1 hour until the juice is running. Strain and squeeze out all the juice. Measure the liquid and allow 350 g/12 oz/1½ cups of sugar to each 600 ml/1 pt/2½ cups of liquid. Boil the sugar and juice together rapidly for 5 minutes, straining off any scum. Bottle, seal and sterilise as for bottled fruit, or freeze in polythene containers.

Use this syrup with ice cream, diluting it if it is too strong or too sweet. Serve with cold water or soda water as a summer drink, or with hot water for a cold. Use as a syrup for fresh fruit salad.

Rose Syrup

Makes about 1.2 litres/2 pts/5 cups

	Metric	Imperial	American
Rose petals	200	200	200
Water	1.2 litres	2 pts	5 cups
Sugar	450 g	1 lb	2 cups

You will need about 35 fresh roses for this, and dark richly-scented red ones are the best. Cut the little white point from each petal as this is bitter. Boil the water and sugar together for 2 minutes. Add rose petals and simmer gently for 30 minutes. Leave to stand overnight, then simmer again for 15 minutes. Strain into small jars and store in the fridge.

You can use this for flavouring sponge cakes, and the leftover pulp can be used as a filling for a sandwich cake. The syrup is good with gin and hot water for a cold. Red roses are supposed to have medicinal properties.

You can use 200 violets in the same amount of sugar and water for Violet Syrup.

Lemonade

Makes about 2 litres/3 ½ pts/8 ½ cups

	Metric	Imperial	American
Lemons	2	2	2
Orange	1	1	1
Water	900 ml	1 ½ pts	3 ¾ cups
Sugar	750 g	1 ½ lb	3 cups
Tartaric acid	90 ml	6 tbsp	6 tbsp

Peel the fruit very thinly and boil the peel in the water for 5 minutes. Strain and pour over the sugar and strained fruit juice. Boil again and stir in the tartaric acid. Bottle and store in the fridge.

Dilute to taste. This is refreshing when served in hot weather, but it can also be used with boiling water as a nightcap for a cold.

Fruit Vinegar

Use raspberries, loganberries, blackberries or blackcurrants. Cover the fruit with white vinegar and mash it each day for 4 or 5 days, stirring well. Strain and measure the juice and allow 450 g/1 lb/ 2 cups sugar to each 600 ml/1 pt/2½ cups juice. Boil for 10 minutes and put into bottles.

Dilute with cold water or soda for a summer drink, or add boiling water for a nightcap. Children were often given raspberry vinegar for colds. In Yorkshire, they use fruit vinegar as a tasty sauce for plain suet and rice puddings.

FARMHOUSE SPECIALS

Of necessity, old country farmers used to preserve may more things than we do now. What's more, not a thing was wasted. As well as making jams, jellies, chutneys and pickles from local fruits and vegetables, they would have stores of bottled produce of all kinds to last them through the winter.

As they raised their own livestock, this too had to be preserved so that nothing went to waste. Sheepskins were cured; the fat rendered down and whipped with rosewater to make hand creams. Even the leftover bits of fat and skin were rendered down and used to waterproof boots and keep leather soft and supple, or added to other ingredients to make soap.

This chapter includes just a few old-fashioned specialities that may be fun to make, even though they are not essential now so many other preserving methods – and supermarkets! – are open to us!

The range of sweets we can buy is almost overwhelming, but there is still nothing quite like the taste of genuine home-made toffee.

Pork Sausages

Makes about 450 g/1 lb

	Metric	Imperial	American
Pork	450 g	1 lb	1 lb
Breadcrumbs	100 g	4 oz	¼ lb
Salt and pepper			
Pinch of sage or marjoram			

Use pork which is half fat and half lean. Put
through the mincer. Soak the breadcrumbs in
cold water then squeeze them almost dry. Mix
with the meat and season well. Either fill
sausage skins with a hand-filler, or with an
attachment on an electric mincer, or just form the
mixture into sausage shapes. Keep in the fridge
or freeze them for later use.

Pork Pie

Serves 4

	Metric	Imperial	American
Plain (all-purpose) flour	450 g	1 lb	4 cups
Lard	150 g	5 oz	⅔ cup
Salt	2.5 ml	½ tsp	½ tsp
Boiling water			
Pork	450 g	1 lb	1 lb
Salt and pepper			

Rub the lard into the flour, add salt and mix with a little boiling water. Knead well and leave on one side for 1 hour, but do not let it get cold. Mould a pie shape over the end of a jam jar, getting the walls of an even thickness. Cut the pork into very small pieces, or mince it. Season well and put into the pastry case. Add a spoonful of water. Put on a pastry lid and pinch the edges together. Make a hole in the centre and decorate with leaves of pastry. Brush all over with a little egg beaten with a pinch of salt. Bake in a preheated oven at 220°C/425°F/gas mark 7 for 20 minutes, then at 180°C/350°F/gas mark 4 for 1 hour. Cover the pastry if it is getting too brown. Meanwhile, simmer any pork bones or trimmings in a little water to make a rich stock. Leave until it has almost turned to jelly. Pour a little into the hole in the lid when the pie comes out of the oven, and then when the pie is cold the jelly should be set.

Beef Roll

Serves 6

	Metric	Imperial	American
Lean beef	600 g	1 ¼ lb	1 ¼ cups
Bacon	450 g	1 lb	1 lb
Breadcrumbs	225 g	8 oz	½ lb
Salt and pepper			
Egg, beaten	1	1	1
Hard-boiled eggs	2	2	2

Mince together the beef, bacon and breadcrumbs. Season well and bind with the beaten egg. Flatten out to a square and put the hard-boiled eggs in the middle. Roll up into a neat cylinder. Wrap in greased paper and then steam for 2 hours. Remove paper and cool, and if liked dust with browned breadcrumbs.

This is good to 'cut and come again' in summer or winter.

Pressed Beef

Serves 6

	Metric	Imperial	American
Beef brisket	1.5 kg	3 lb	3 lb
Salt and pepper			
Gelatine	15 ml	1 tbsp	1 tbsp

Roll the brisket and tie it into shape. Put the beef into a pan, cover with water and season well. Bring to the boil, skim, and then simmer gently for 4 hours until tender. Cool slightly and then put into a basin or large mould. Put a plate on top and a weight to press it down. Strain the liquid and measure out 450 ml/¾ pint/2 cups liquid. Stir the gelatine into a little of the liquid and dissolve over heat until the gelatine is syrupy. Add to the measured liquid and pour over the meat. Leave until set and jellied. Tongue can also be prepared in this way too.

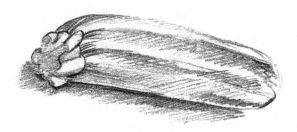

Meat Glaze

Makes about 150 ml/¼ pt/⅔ cup

	Metric	Imperial	American
Stock	150 ml	¼ pint	⅔ cup
Beef cube	1	1	1
Gelatine	7.5 ml	½ tbsp	½ tbsp

Dissolve the beef cube in the stock and stir in the gelatine. Heat gently and keep stirring until liquid is smooth and clear. Season to taste with salt and pepper. Brush over any cold meat and allow to set, then brush over again, using two or three 'coats'. The glaze should be cool when used and may be used to coat any cooked meat.

Hinderwell Toffee

Makes about 225 g/8 oz

	Metric	Imperial	American
Butter	150 g	5 oz	⅔ cup
Sugar	150 g	5 oz	⅔ cup
Golden (light corn) syrup	50 g	2 oz	4 tbsp
Single (light) cream	30 ml	2 tbsp	2 tbsp

Beat together the butter and sugar as if making a cake and work in the syrup and cream. Stir well and then boil for 20 minutes. Pour into a buttered tin, cool, and then cut into squares and wrap in paper.

Leadgate Toffee

Makes about 225 g/8 oz

	Metric	Imperial	American
Butter	100 g	4 oz	½ cup
Sugar	175 g	6 oz	¾ cup
Vinegar	45 ml	3 tbsp	3 tbsp
Golden (light corn) syrup	45 ml	3 tbsp	3 tbsp
Water	30 ml	2 tbsp	2 tbsp
Lemon essence (extract)			

Put all the ingredients into a pan and stir over low heat until the sugar has dissolved. Boil fast for 6 minutes and pour into a greased tin. Break in pieces when cold.

Peggy's Toffee

Makes about 225 g/8 oz

	Metric	Imperial	American
Butter	175 g	6 oz	¾ cup
Sugar	450 g	1 lb	2 cups
Vinegar	60 ml	4 tbsp	4 tbsp

Melt the butter and stir in the sugar. Dissolve over low heat, then add vinegar and stir until it boils. Boil hard for 6 minutes and then pour into a greased tin. Break in pieces when cold. Never stir after it boils.

Stanhope Toffee

Makes about 900 g/2 lb

	Metric	Imperial	American
Almonds, halved	50 g	2 oz	½ cup
Sugar	450 g	1 lb	2 cups
Butter	100 g	4 oz	½ cup
Single (light) cream	15 ml	1 tbsp	1 tbsp
Condensed milk	30 ml	2 tbsp	2 tbsp
Golden (light corn) syrup	30 ml	2 tbsp	2 tbsp
Vinegar	30 ml	2 tbsp	2 tbsp

Finely chop half of the almonds and put these and all the other ingredients into a pan and stir until the sugar has dissolved. Bring to the boil and do not stir again. Boil rapidly for 5 minutes. Pour into a greased tin. Arrange the remaining almonds on top of the toffee and leave until cold before breaking into pieces.

USEFUL HOUSEHOLD RECIPES

Many herbs can be grown in the garden and they are so useful.

Mint is cut in our garden in August or September and dried in the kitchen inside a paper bag to keep the dust off. I rub off the dry crackly leaves just before Christmas and keep them in a tightly lidded jar. You can use these dried leaves for mint tea, which is believed to be very good for colic and wind in the stomach.

Sage is treated in the same way as mint, and is very useful for sage and onion stuffing with a winter joint of pork, or a fat duck or goose.

Marjoram is my favourite herb for puddings, stuffings and sausages, and I dry it the same way when the flowers have just finished.

Lavender is good burned on a shovel to drive out offensive smells, and it leaves a lovely fragrance.

Marigolds used to be used a lot. You just dry the flowers and add them to soup, salads or cream cheese. You don't need much, but they are very tasty.

Honey and Lemon Soother

Makes about 250 ml/8 fl oz/1 cup

	Metric	Imperial	American
Cod liver oil	50 ml	2 fl oz	3 ½ tbsp
Honey	50 g	2 oz	4 tbsp
Juice of lemons	4	4	4

Shake all the ingredients together and take to soothe a cough. Do not drink too much as the cod liver oil could upset the stomach.

Lemon and Brown Sugar Balm

Makes about 600 ml/1 pt/2 ½ cups

	Metric	Imperial	American
Brown sugar	30 ml	2 tbsp	2 tbsp
Juice of lemons	2	2	2
Olive oil	15 ml	1 tbsp	1 tbsp
Boiling water	600 ml	1 pt	2½ cups

Add the water to the other ingredients and stir well until dissolved. Put into a bottle, and give one tablespoon of the mixture to soothe a cough.

Mincemeat

Makes about 3.5 kg/8 lb

	Metric	Imperial	American
Apples	1.5 kg	3 lb	3 lb
Raisins, chopped	450 g	1 lb	2 ⅔ cups
Currants	225 g	8 oz	1 ⅓ cups
Shredded suet	450 g	1 lb	4 cups
Sugar	750 g	1 ½ lb	3 cups
Chopped mixed peel	100 g	4 oz	⅔ cup
Ground nutmeg	5 ml	1 tsp	1 tsp
Ground mixed spice	5 ml	1 tsp	1 tsp
Grated rind of lemon	1	1	1

Peel, core and chop the apples. Mix all the ingredients together and put into screw-top preserving jars. Keep in a cool place.

I usually make this a couple of weeks before Christmas. Sometimes I add a few chopped almonds and you can put in some brandy, sherry or rum.

Breadcrumbs

Home-made fresh or dried breadcrumbs are far nicer than the often orange-coloured ones on the supermarket shelves. They are useful for all kinds of things in the kitchen. Put stale bread crusts through the mincer or food processor and then dry them for a few minutes in the oven before storing. You can also make crumbs by grating bread and drying the crumbs in the oven.

Use in a plum pudding or suet pudding to make them lighter, or keep them on hand for fruit Charlottes. I find them very useful for coating food which is to be fried.

Pot Pourri

Gather flowers on a dry calm day, and use such perfumed flowers and leaves as rose petals, lavender, thyme, verbena and stock. Spread on paper or a rack in a dry place and turn the petals often so they dry. Put into a jar and sprinkle clean dry cooking salt between each layer. Stand in a dry place for 2 weeks. Add 25 g/1 oz/2 tbsp cloves, 25 g/1 oz/2 tbsp cinnamon stick, 25 g/1 oz/ 2 tbsp allspice and a little grated nutmeg. Cover with a close-fitting lid. Sprinkle with a little orange-flower water or eau-de-cologne if liked. This will keep fragrant for years, but should only be left open for 30 minutes each day.

FREEZING

Freezing is now a popular way of preserving food, and it is a very useful way of keeping fruit, vegetables and meat in particular. I also like to keep some of my cooked dishes and cakes ready for unexpected visitors.

Vegetables
Always freeze small quantities of vegetables at a time, fresh from the garden to preserve their goodness. I like to pick early in the day and prepare the vegetables when I am getting some ready for our midday meal.

I use a big saucepan for preparing the vegetables and a wire basket. The saucepan holds about 5 litres/9 pints/22 cups of water and I bring it to the boil, then put in 450 g/1 lb of prepared vegetables. Then the lid goes on and the water has to come back to the boil quickly. As soon as it boils, I start timing. Most vegetables only need 1-2 minutes cooking (or blanching) like this. Then they go straight into iced water, because running tap water just isn't cold enough. When they are chilled, I dry them on kitchen paper and pack straight into polythene bags or boxes for freezing. You can prepare most vegetables in this way, but I think peas and beans are the nicest. Small young carrots can be good, and of course sprouts, but I don't bother to freeze many other green or root vegetables, which anyway keep longer in the garden I always prepare a few bags of tomatoes because they are so useful for cooking in the winter. They don't need any special treatment, and I just wipe them and pack them into bags for freezing.

Fruit

Soft fruits can soften in the freezer but are still perfect for cooking. I usually just put berries or currants into bags and freeze them without sugar as they are so much more useful afterwards. If I have a lot of fruit and not much space, I cook it first and then make it into sweet purée for freezing. You can freeze fruit in dry sugar too, or in syrup, but that takes longer and I don't think there is much point as it can be cooked and sweetened later. Apples need sugar or syrup though, or they will discolour, and the same goes for peaches and apricots.

Meat, Poultry and Game

Prepare meat and poultry before freezing and pack it in the quantities you are most likely to use. Pack meat or poultry into polythene and take out all the air. It is important to freeze these things quickly for the best results. It is essential that meat and poultry are thawed thoroughly before cooking.

When I feel like cooking a lot, I make a few extra things for the freezer. Mostly I freeze stews and soups which I usually put into foil containers which can be used for reheating. Pies and puddings freeze well too, and don't take long to reheat. I like to keep a few cakes in the freezer – scones are very useful, and one or two sponge and butter-iced cakes, while a few loaves of bread are a good standby. They only need wrapping in polythene and freezing quickly.

There really aren't many rules about freezing. I find it is important to be very clean and to keep everything cool in the kitchen. All air has to come out of packages, and it is important to freeze food quickly for good results. Vegetables don't need thawing before cooking but everything else is best thawed slowly in the fridge.

Index

Mary Ford.